# LOSING TINA

## TINA

INGRID HELSELL JARVIS

This book is dedicated to my sister Kristina Myra Helsell, who gave me love, protection, laughter, and a lifetime of precious memories, and to anyone who suffers from debilitating depression.

## TABLE OF CONTENTS

## Part 1: Growing Up Helsell

## Part 2: Tina (1986–2014)

## Part Three: My Road Back (2015–present)

I have always been an avid reader. I thank my parents Robert and Linda Helsell for this gift. My favorite authors are Pearl Buck, Wallace Stegner, Isabel Allende, and Lauren Groff. They bring people and places to life so beautifully. Their stories have inspired me to bring my family and, specifically, Tina to these pages. May she come alive in your mind and heart.

# PREFACE

Since childhood, my brilliant older sister, Tina, was plagued by mental illness. One day, she couldn't fight the battle anymore. It has been seven years since she took her life on New Year's Eve, 2014. My family was finishing up our post-Christmas holiday in our home in La Quinta, California. The five of us had enjoyed a late New Year's dinner, and everyone went their separate ways. My husband, Eric, was out on our patio with our sons, Henry and George. I was snuggled in our bed with a glass of wine and a great Netflix series. Our daughter, Hazel, was in her room, most likely Snapchatting her girlfriends. At about 11:00 p.m., my husband came into our room. He shut the door behind him, hung his head low, and let out a big, sad sigh. My initial reaction was that something was wrong with our children, but I realized they were all there. I asked, "Eric what is wrong?" He hesitated and said, "Your dad has been trying to reach us. Your sister killed herself."

When you hear that your best friend in the world, who was also your sister, decided to violently end her life, there are no words. The moment is suspended. Everything stops. As I noted in my reading at Tina's memorial service, "When your life comes to a complete and shocking stop, everything still keeps going. Siblings still fight, there are dishes to do and groceries to buy, and your spouse wants so badly to see you smile. Friends are crucial and so amazing. People who have experienced tragedy bravely reach out and want to share."

It has taken me this long to even think about putting my grief into words. Instead of focusing on the deep sorrow, now I want to celebrate her. I want everyone to know about this extraordinary woman who had talent, brains, beauty, and humor. This memoir is about the very special relationship I had with Tina and the inevitable disintegration of our bond

1

as her mental illness became more acute. It's also the story of how survivors like me and others in our family find ways to continue their lives and reach out to others who have lost dear ones to suicide.

I dedicate this book to anyone on this planet who suffers from mental illness. It is a cruel, silent condition that is finally gaining recognition in the medical world. It needs to be taken as seriously as diabetes, cancer, and heart disease.

# Part 1: Growing Up Helsell

CHAPTER 1

# Family Background

Tina cannot be understood unless I share our family history, starting with both sets of grandparents and, specifically, what it meant to be raised by a mother with mental illness. Our family background is a bit of a wild ride. The history of mental illness on our maternal side shaped my grandparents, Mom and the four of us, and affected Tina the most intensely. Our paternal side was much less tinged with mental illness, but there was an absence of emotional connection from our paternal grandparents that shaped my father and dribbled down to each of us in various forms. When I look back at our maternal grandparents and their behaviors and then at my mom, it's no wonder that we children were affected. As you will see later, being the oldest was a hard position for Tina to be in. She had to forge the way, and with an unpredictable and unstable mother, it was always an uphill battle.

Four seems to be the magic number in the Clark and Helsell families. Mom's family was from Calgary, Alberta. Her parents, Myra and Spencer Clark, had four children: our mom, Linda, her brothers, Joe and Charlie, and sister, Maggie. Mom was the oldest, then Joe, and then twelve years later, they had Maggie, closely followed by Charlie. They had two older and two younger kids. My father's parents, Frank and Ellen Helsell, had four children. Our dad, Robert, was the youngest sibling by thirteen years, so his siblings' birth order followed a similar pattern. He had two older brothers, Jack, followed by Bill, and then a sister, Ruth. Dad was thirteen years younger than Ruth. My parents had four children, Tina, followed by me seventeen months later, Spencer, four years my junior, and then eleven years later, my sister Alexa. All three families had four children, with significant age differences between the oldest and youngest.

Linda Clark's household was chaotic and filled with energy and some rage. Myra was completely deaf until my mom was seven years old when surgery restored her hearing. Hence, my grandmother couldn't hear Linda and Joe for the first part of their childhood, where bonds are formed and nurtured. Her inability to hear most certainly made her frustrated. Mom's recollection of her childhood is very painful, and in my lifetime, I never heard her say a kind thing about her mom. One of Mom's distinct memories is from first grade. She said, "My mom was supposed to bake and prepare the cookies for my class that week. She just didn't do it. It was embarrassing and humiliating. I was little." I used to think that memory was silly, but after I became a mother of three and had those responsibilities, I understood. My kids would light up every time I showed up in their elementary classrooms, whether it was with birthday treats for the class, to volunteer for a class party, or help the teacher in the classroom.

Both Spencer and Myra had tempers. They would erupt over the smallest things: a grandchild breaking a glass, being too loud, not making our beds properly when staying with them. My grandfather would call us "boobs" when he was displeased with us. One time, I was practicing my piano music at their house. When I was finished, my grandfather said, "Ingrid, you shouldn't play the piano if you are not good enough to accompany someone. And you are not!" Those moments brought me to tears and, as I got older, I started to wonder what it might have been like to be raised in that home.

Conversely, my father's home was a gentle, quiet place to be raised. His mother, Ellen Helsell, was from Plainview, Nebraska, and his father, Frank, was raised in Odebolt, Iowa. Ellen was the most peaceful, lovely grandmother. She was an active member of her community, and she co-founded the Episcopalian church called St. Thomas in Medina, Washington. Ellen also loved to bake cookies. Our dad, Robert, being the baby, was raised by his parents, but they also had a lot of help from Mrs. Gleason, Dad's nanny.

I don't remember my grandfather Frank at all. He got Parkinson's disease in his late seventies, and he died when I was two years old. There is a story about him that I find most impressive. Our dad went to Dartmouth College. He studied hard and got very good grades his freshman year. When he was a sophomore, he was busy rowing for the crew team, meeting new friends, and being part of a fraternity. In those days, the college sent the grades home, so the parents saw them first. One day, he was walking across campus, and a gentleman was walking toward him. As they got closer, he realized it was his father. Frank Helsell had flown from Seattle to New Hampshire three thousand miles across the country. Dad asked, "Dad, what are you doing here?!" He said, "Robert, you have C's and a D on your report card, and your mother and I are concerned. Are you OK?" Dad replied, "Yes, I am great! I guess I have been having too much fun rowing and meeting new friends." That trip showed my grandfather's moral character and in turn, my father towed the line. He finished strong at Dartmouth, and became an excellent role model for us, especially in terms of studies.

I have fond memories of Easter at Frank and Ellen's home. Mom dressed Tina and me up in pink and light blue wool jackets, with matching skirts and bonnets. They always put on a large Easter egg hunt followed by brunch. Ellen eventually remarried. I do remember going to visit her and her husband John Paul when I was in my teens. She always had fresh cookies for us and a huge smile. I used to love to kiss her soft cheek. She was quiet and a listener. Our dad was always sweet around my grandmother, but they weren't very affectionate. I sensed an emotional void, even when I was younger. She developed dementia when I was in my early teens, and she died when I was 16. So, on the one hand, we were molded and shaped by my mother's dislike of her mother and by their family's chaos and anger. On the other hand, we inherited gentleness and peacefulness from my father's side, albeit lacking tangible emotional connections. Unfortunately, the stormy side prevailed. Spencer was diagnosed as bipolar in his fifties.

Toward the end of his life, he carried around a simple black box, declaring it held all the secrets of the universe. My mom was diagnosed as bipolar in her mid-forties.

Generally, we spent much more time with our mom's family than with our dad's. Looking back, it would have been beneficial to have more of their influence, especially Jack Helsell's, his wife Jan and their three daughters, our cousins, Mary Jane, Susie, and Ellen. Mom's anger, unpredictability, drug use, and lack of parenting in our teen years led all four of us to have mental health issues. Tina's were the most severe and resulted in her tragic decision to end her life.

Thanks to our incredibly hardworking father, we had money. We were fortunate in that way. My father purchased the home we grew up in from his parents when Tina and I were two and three years old, so from early childhood, we lived in a beautiful craftsman-style home on two acres, on the shores of Lake Washington. Dad was an avid sailor, and we owned a forty-foot sloop called *Bohemia,* which lived at the end of our dock. We were able to take sailing trips to the San Juan Islands in Washington State and to Desolation Sound in British Columbia, Canada. We were skiers, and we co-owned a little condominium with another family at Crystal Mountain ski resort, where we all learned to ski. Back then, Mom was passionate about skiing, far more than Dad. Our parents were very good friends with a couple named Peter and Sally Jarvis. Before they both had children, Sally and our mom taught ski lessons together. The Jarvises had four children, Scot, Eric, Molly, and Dwight. They were and are a remarkably talented family. All four children are athletic, bright, hardworking, and blessed with eye-catching physiques. One time when Tina and I were getting off a chairlift, we saw Scot and Eric Jarvis, the two oldest boys, both impossibly handsome. They were excellent skiers and so nice to Tina and me. But we were so intimidated by them because they were much better skiers. Tina said, "Ing, "quick, let's go the other way! It's the Jarvis brothers." Fast forward fourteen years. I started dating Eric Jarvis and fell in love. We have been married for twenty-eight years.

Our dad was in the construction business for forty years. As his income grew, we took yearly trips to Hawaii, from high school on. Despite the fact that he was a big earner, Mom constantly worried about money. There was never enough to satisfy her. Of course, the construction industry ebbs and flows. During ebbs, Mom would say, "I wish your father was in the underwear industry because everyone always needs underwear!" It wasn't rational because we never wanted for much. I never really understood her fear. Sadly, her relationship with money passed on to Tina, who was also anxious about money throughout her life. When Tina and her husband Bill went through financially hard times in their mid-forties, she lost all sense of security. This also contributed to her downfall. Tina, Spencer, and I were raised in the '60s and '70s when there was not a lot of open discussion about anxiety and depression, nor were people talking much about therapy and seeking it out. I think if Tina had been born a generation later, she would still be alive.

# CHAPTER 2

# Childhood (1966–1976)

W hen I look book at our early childhood, I recall mostly love, laughter, and companionship with Tina, sprinkled with fighting and feistiness. My first memories of her revolve around being outside. My earliest image of us together is driving our bright red toy fire engines around our patio. Our patio extended from the living room, and the railings were black wrought iron. We were paddling our cars with our feet and giggling, delighting in crashing into each other. In the summer, while Mom worked in her vegetable garden, we would snack on the blueberries Mom grew, play in our tree fort that Dad built, swim in the lake, and play in the woods that bordered our driveway. This was the '60s; there were no cell phones. Most people didn't even have an answering machine. If I phoned my best friend Margot, who lived down the street, and kept getting a busy signal, I'd read, play on my own, or track down Tina, who was always my preferred playmate. There was this old stone chimney located at the edge of the woods near our driveway. It must have been the remnant of a small old house that had existed years ago. We called it the witch's stove, and it was the perfect spot for creating mud pies out of twigs, leaves, dirt, and water.

Our neighbors to the north were Dick and Betty Warner. Tina and I used to love visiting the Warners when we were little. They must have been in their early fifties when we were young; their children were out of college. Betty would give us lemonade and cookies in the summertime. Dick was a different story. He was bald, quirky, and had a scary laugh. He used to say, "Hey girls, you know about the ogre who lives in the woods, don't you? You have to be good little girls, or he'll get you!" There was a patch of woods we shared with the Warners, separating our driveways. Tina and I had to walk past the ogre zone to and from our bus stop. To the south of us were the Clines. All I remember about them was that Mrs. Cline was incredibly crabby, always had a sour look on her face, and had an ongoing dispute with my parents about a large tree that bordered both our properties. Needless to say, there were no cookies and lemonade from them, ever.

I also remember Mom having tea parties with Tina and me on our side lawn, near a big maple tree. She would turn milk into different colors using food coloring, and Tina and I would choose a color to be. I would choose red, and Tina green, and Mom would say, "So Miss Green, how are you today and what would you like to discuss?" Mom was very imaginative when we were little. Our birthday parties were almost always at home. Mom made the multicolored milk and wrote her own Mad Libs. In them, she included every single girl, so there was much laughter.

One of my most distinct memories of Tina was an incident involving a doll. Tina, Margot, and I were watching TV downstairs on a Saturday afternoon. Dad came into the room and said, "Girls, your mom is taking a nap, and you are not to disturb her." We all nodded and went back to our show. About halfway through the episode, I really, really wanted a baby doll that was in a closet in Mom and Dad's room. I went upstairs and snuck as quietly as I could into their room. Either the opening of the closet door or my not-so-graceful sneaking woke Mom up. Dad was furious. He sent Margot home and asked Tina and me who had woken her up. Neither of us fessed up, and he ended up spanking Tina right in front of me. In those days, we were spanked on our butts by Dad's hand or Mom's wooden spoon. I will never ever forget the guilt I felt watching Tina take my punishment, knowing she was feeling pain for something I did. It was an indelible memory because I worshipped her. I think she endured the spanking because she didn't want me to hurt. It was her pride in being the oldest, the child who stood up for me, Spencer, and Alexa. She was my protector. That was forty-eight years ago, and I remember it like it was yesterday.

Another example of her protection involved an incident in elementary school. Tina and I both attended Three Points Elementary School, from kindergarten through grade five. When we were in the lower grades, we took the school bus that picked us up in front of our driveway. In grades four and five, we walked from home to school, which was at least one and a half miles to and from. On really rainy days, Mom would pick us up. The walk consisted of walking all the way down our street (called Hunts Point), and then crossing an overpass over the 520 highway that led into Seattle. The overpass ended right in front of the school.

One day after school, Tina and I crossed the overpass and then walked down the path that led to our street. As we were walking down the path, I turned up and saw Ed and Tammy. Tammy and Ed were the only "couple" in the fifth grade. They were always together. They held hands and even kissed. Imagine me for a second, a third-grader, a little chubby, with an unflattering bowl cut. At the top of my lungs, I yelled at them, "Ed and Tammy, sitting in a tree, K I S S I NG. First comes love, then comes marriage, then comes the baby in the baby carriage!" At about "First comes love," Ed dropped his backpack on the overpass and ran like a cheetah toward us. I was beyond terrified. Tina grabbed my hand and said, "Well, Ing, that was really, really dumb." As Ed approached us, all red-faced and angry, Tina stood in front of me to shield me. He got close to us and said, "I am going to hit your little sister." Tina replied, "Ed, please don't. She didn't mean it. She was just being dumb." It took Ed a while to calm down, but he did, thanks to Tina. At that point, Tammy had joined us, holding both of their backpacks, sneering at me. I can't imagine what would have happened if I had been walking without Tina and decided to sing that little ditty.

Like most younger siblings, I looked up to Tina and wanted to be just like her. Our mom used to dress us alike in Christmas outfits, summer dresses, even matching bathing suits. When Tina was about six, she announced, "I do not want to dress like Ingrid anymore. I want to wear clothes that are different from hers." I was devastated. From that day forward, she wouldn't even consider the same pattern. I tried for a while to continue the twin look, but she was adamant.

We developed secret languages together and both loved to mimic voices. Our family loved to watch the *Carol Burnett Show*. Tim Conway's sketch "Mrs. A Wiggins" was one of our favorites. Tim Conway had an assistant named Mrs. Wiggins, played by Carol Burnett. She was lazy. Tim had a Swedish accent, and he would say, "Mrs. A Viggins, if you aren't a too busy, vould you a please come into my office and take a some dictation." Tina could mimic him perfectly. When she started with "My name is Mrs. A Viggins," I would instantly start laughing.

Tina also had an incredible aptitude for languages and accents. She could manipulate her voice into most octaves and could mimic any foreign accent, as well as imitate actors we watched on TV. It's no surprise that she developed a gift for learning languages as she grew up, first French and then Mandarin. (Our oldest son, Henry, has the same talent, and for years, he and Tina would make each other laugh heartily with their accents and impressions.)

On long car rides, Tina and I would sit on opposite sides of the car, turn toward each other slowly, and glare until one of us made the other laugh. There were no TVs in cars or noise-canceling earphones. We had to create our entertainment. And, I was lucky to have such a funny older sister who initiated most of the game-playing. Just another reason to worship her.

When Tina was five and I was four, our brother, John Spencer Helsell, was born on January 12, 1969. Spencer was a quiet and sweet little boy. There is a picture of me holding him in a bassinet outside, near a big cherry tree. He was sleeping, and I remember that I loved watching him. When he was a little older, he would spend hours in his room, building big cities out of Legos. He was methodical and smart, and we adored him. We especially liked to dress him up in girls' clothes. He was quieter than Tina and me, and because there was an age gap between him and us, it was more like we were a team and he was on his own. His best friend in the world was Steve Hoedemaker. They would spend full days together, at our home or theirs. Tina's best childhood friend was Steve's sister Linda. Tina and Spence shared a lot with their love for the Hoedemaker family.

David and Ivaly Hoedemaker were dear friends of my parents. They lived across the lake from us in a neighborhood called Yarrow Point. Their three children are John, Linda, and Steve. Because Tina had Linda, and Spencer had Steve, John and I were on the periphery; he was the oldest, and I was the middle child, with no matchup in age. David is an architect, and he designed their contemporary home. I loved it because it was so different from ours. Ours was an old colonial with rigid lines and well-defined rooms. We had lots of antique, dark furniture. Their home was more open, light-filled, and had modern touches, like cool lighting and comfy couches. David was always kind and had a great laugh. Ivaly was the most lovely, gentle, graceful, kind woman. She called me "grid." That was my nickname growing up. My uncle Charlie gave me the nickname "grid city" when I was about seven. I never really liked it, but I tolerated the shorter version "grid." For some reason, it didn't bother me when Ivaly or her family called me "grid." She was tall, thin, and lithe. Linda is a beautiful replica of her mother, in every way.

My family was loud, and the Hoedemakers were quieter and more reserved. Linda describes the differences between her and Tina as "black and white." Whereas Tina was funny, loud, irreverent, Linda was quiet, graceful, and polite. But they just worked together. I think Tina loved Linda's gentle nature, and Linda loved Tina's humor and spunk. They were a good example of opposites attract. They also loved each other's mothers for the qualities they didn't get from their own mothers: Ivaly's unconditional love for Tina, and Mom's openness and honesty toward Linda.

Linda has very fond memories of being at our home, and she loved Mom. One Halloween, Linda was dressed as a Native American. As Mom applied Linda's face paint, a few tears ran down Linda's cheeks. She said, "I don't have pretty eyes like Tina and Ingrid." My Mom took her face in her hands and said, "Linda, you are so beautiful." Linda remembers that as the first time she felt pretty. Mom made her feel special, just as Ivaly did for Tina.

In 1971, the Hoedemakers bought a spectacular piece of property on Lopez Island, which is part of the beautiful San Juan Islands archipelago in Washington State. The property had a large farmhouse, a big barn, and wheat fields that reached out to a private beach on Puget Sound. As a family, we were fortunate to spend special weekends there and, naturally, Spencer and Tina spent a great deal of time there. Every year they hosted a big square dance party in their barn, as a way to thank and give back to the Lopez Island community. They invited some of their favorite families that lived not on Lopez but back in our home city of Bellevue. I remember those square dances as a flurry of cowboy boots, hats, square dancing, and lots of hay everywhere. I have allergies, two of them being horses and hay. So for me, the square dances weren't great, but for the rest of my family, they were one of the highlights of the summer.

Whenever Tina returned from Lopez, she was sad. Being there with Linda and her family was always very special for her because, I think, Tina was more comfortable with their family than she was with us, especially during her teenage years. Ivaly's death in 2005 had a devastating impact on our family as well as her own, and especially on Tina and Mom. Linda and Tina remained dear friends.

We had a lot of chores growing up. One of them was deadheading hundreds of dead rhododendron blooms. When the blooms die, you have to snap them off the stem just right, and they get so sticky that your garden gloves get sticky and unusable. There were probably fifty rhododendron bushes on our property. While I worked, Tina decided her job was to entertain me. She would sing along to the transistor radio, dancing, cracking jokes. I just kept deadheading while she got out of it, every time. It used to make me so mad. I'd say, "Tina, this is so unfair. Why am I doing all the work?" She would put her hands on her hip and say, "Ingrid, I am funnier than you are and a better entertainer, and you are a better worker." I would try and tell Mom about it, but she always ignored me. She really only cared that the jobs got done, not about the division of labor.

Cutting back ferns in early fall was another dreaded chore. The ferns were at the edge of the woods alongside the driveway. I had to use big shears and cut the ferns back, so the new baby fronds would appear. Ferns can be scratchy, and if I was wearing a tee shirt, I could get scraped up. Sometimes Tina would just leave. I don't know if she went to her room or hid out in the house, but after the ferns were cut, I'd come back to the house fuming, dirty and wanting to smack her. I will give Tina credit; she was creative in her defiance of daily chores. Later in life, she didn't have her daughters do chores because she hated them. The irony is she did have a tremendous work ethic when it came to her schoolwork, career, and volunteer work. When she enjoyed the work, she worked hard.

Just because you worship someone, doesn't mean that you don't have an occasional "moment." The cruelest thing I ever did to Tina happened on a camping trip. It was a father/child trip for a two-day overnight near Mt. Rainier. We were six and seven years old, and we went with three other families. My family didn't really camp that much, and we had the worst, most outdated gear. Dad, Tina, and I had to sleep in an old, two-man army tent, while the others were in spacious REI family tents. We were freezing at night because we had these little kid sleeping bags with defective insulation. Also, Dad brought the worst food along, and Tina and I were envious of the others' dinners. One afternoon, Tina and I went to a private spot to go to the bathroom. I peed, but she had to poop. About an hour later, all the kids were playing together, and I said, "Hey, do you guys want me to show you where Tina pooped? You can see her poop." "Sure!" they exclaimed. Tina turned white as a ghost. I led the other seven kids over to the poop spot, a mossy area behind a log. Tina was devastated, and Dad was very angry with me. I still feel shame that I did that.

Some of the most magical moments of our childhood were when we visited our grandparents, Myra and Spencer Clark. Even though Gaga and Grandpa were challenging, we loved spending weekends with them. The physical beauty of their home and property would have been special for any child. My grandparents lived in an exclusive gated community in North Seattle called the Highlands. Their home was built by Roland Terry, a famous architect. It was modern and spacious and filled with light. Their spectacular view took in Puget Sound flanked by the Olympic Mountains.

They collected works by famous Northwest artists, threw huge parties, and drank excessively. Money and status were very important to both of them, as it came to be for our mother and, eventually, Tina.

I remember my grandfather, Charles Spencer Clark, as a very bright, intense man. Grandpa used to read all of the time. He balanced his reading glasses on his nose. He was a smoker and had a constant cough. He didn't like excess noise, so sometimes having Tina and me there together was too much. Occasionally, I would spend a weekend there alone, and so would Tina, but it was always more fun when we were there together.

Our grandmother was as beautiful as Grandpa was bright. We called her "Gaga," and she could've out-glammed the superstar of the same name. She was blonde with piercing blue eyes. Her style was unmatched and her jewelry exquisite. She would go from wearing colorful, exotic caftans one day to a tailored Chanel suit the next. She hummed to herself a lot. She called me "Ingie Boo" and always stroked my face because she loved my soft skin. Her bathroom was enormous, and she had a hairdryer that you used to see in salons. She would roll our hair into big curlers and let Tina and I sit under the dryer. She also let us play with the clothes in her expansive closets. But for all her allure, she could lose her temper easily. If I had to go to the bathroom, she would always say, "Ingie Boo, your bottom is so small that you only need to use one square of toilet paper." She would be annoyed if I used more, and I always thought that was strange, given their opulence.

They had a swimming pool and a pond with big croaking frogs. There was a little cart called a "surrey" we pushed around their patio. On Sunday mornings, Gaga always made blueberry pancakes and bacon. Because they both had tempers, Tina and I bonded over being quiet, "good" grand-daughters while in their presence.

Mom's entire family always spent Christmas Eve at their home. These gatherings included Grandpa and Gaga, Mom and Dad, Tina, Spencer, me and eventually Alexa, uncles Joe and Charlie, aunt Maggie and great-uncle Jiggs and his wife, Mary Jane. Jiggs was Grandpa's brother. Joe, Charlie, and Maggie delighted in our little-kid wonder. At that time, they were in their late teens and early twenties. Joe and Maggie never had children. Charlie had one daughter, our beloved cousin Chelsea, who was born two years after Alexa. After dinner, they would sneak around the backside of the house, go up on the roof, and ring bells, as if Santa's sleigh had just landed. Tina, Spencer, and I would shriek in delight. On our drive home, I would still look for Santa's sleigh in the sky.

One Christmas, Joe gave Tina and me life-sized Raggedy Ann and Andy dolls. He gave me Ann and Tina, Andy. When Tina started to cry, Joe asked, "Tina, what's the matter?" She said, "I don't want Andy. I want Ann." I didn't care as much, so I said, "Here Tina. You can have Ann." We were both excited to have dolls that were as big as we were. As we got older, Christmas Eves with our grandparents weren't that great. The only dessert my grandfather liked was a flaming rum pudding, full of dried fruit and booze. So, that's what we had. All the kids only wanted Christmas cookies and ice cream.

For Christmas dinner, we always went to Uncle Jack and Aunt Jan's home. Unlike Christmas Eve with its emotional highs, Christmas evening with Dad's family was always quite subdued. Everyone on Dad's side was polite, kind, and spoke quietly. Also, by that point, Christmas is pretty much over for a kid. The excitement of Christmas Eve is behind you; the presents have been torn open on Christmas morning. I distinctly remember being aware of the differences between both evenings and both families.

An integral part of our early childhood was going to Camp Nor'wester in the summer. Camp Nor'wester was established in 1935. When Tina and I attended, it was located at the edge of Puget Sound on Sperry Peninsula, Lopez Island, on a 387-acre spectacular property. That's where we formed a bond with Aunt Jan and Uncle Jack, who were the camp directors from 1968 to 1980. Our cousins Mary Jane, Susie, and Ellen spent the summers there as well, working at the camp. It was great because if I got homesick, I could go visit Uncle Jack, Aunt Jan, and my cousins. Our parents were wise in that I always attended the first four-week session, and Tina the second four-week session. As close as we were, it was essential that she and I had time apart to meet other friends, and camp was the perfect place for that.

There were many activities, from arts and crafts to archery to a sailing program. I can still remember the smells of camp, the fir trees, the fires from the tipis, and the vats of chicken soup wafting from the lodge. We used to peel the red bark off the Madrona trees, roll them up, and smoke them like cigarettes. The camp was divided into units of similar age groups; each unit had a name, like Weavers, Archers, Pioneers, and Foresters. The younger campers lived in tent platforms, and the older kids lived in tipis. The girls' section of camp was separated from the boys' section by a large, open-aired wooden lodge where we ate all of our meals.

Kwagiutl traditions were an integral part of Nor'wester. The Kwagiutl are the indigenous peoples of the Pacific Northwest Coast. We learned about their traditions, art, and culture. For the second session, there was a Kwagiutl potlatch ceremony. Each camper secretly chose the name of another. They made a special gift for their person, and they exchanged gifts at the ceremony, in a true Native American Lodge, guarded by a totem pole. The camp philosophy was all about taking care of the land, and each other. I believe the spirit of the Kwagiutl was deeply embedded in that land, and their spirits watched over each and every child. Camp Nor'wester was an incredibly magical experience, and many Nor'wester campers went on to be camp counselors there.

Tina attended camp for a few years before I did. I vividly remember her return from Nor'Wester. She would cry and cry and go outside on our porch and cry some more. I didn't understand it until the year I went. When the ferry boat disembarked from Lopez Island, all of us girls cried and cried and hugged each other. The bonds we formed over a month were very tight, and as a unit, we did everything together. To imagine going home without those friends and those shared routines was sad and unnerving. I think my crying was shorter lived than Tina's because she became sad easily.

Much to the dismay of thousands of campers, staff, and the Lopez Island residents, Paul Allen purchased Sperry Peninsula in 1996 for nine million dollars. The camp eventually moved to Johns Island in the San Juans. When our middle child, George, was nine, I urged him and his friend Harry to attend Nor'wester on Johns island. At this point, they had a two-week session option. When I picked George up from the camp bus, I was expecting him to be bursting with excitement and full of stories. Actually, he wasn't overly thrilled. I cannot say, but I wonder if the new property didn't hold that same magic.

However, recently, George (now 23) said, "Mom, Camp Nor'wester was so much fun."

For Tina and me, Camp Nor'wester was definitely a magical experience, and it made our bond stronger because we understood what the other one had experienced. We got the magic. We also bonded over having a sad mom.

# CHAPTER 3

# Middle School (1976–1978)

When Tina turned twelve, her mood and demeanor changed. She was always a bit more serious than me, but a sadness developed. Tina was intense. She brooded and cried a lot. I couldn't really figure out what would set her off. It seemed like the sad mood would just wash over her without warning, and she wouldn't want to talk about it when she was low. There is a photo of her in one of our family albums, sitting in a hammock, eyes bloodshot from crying. Under the picture, the caption says "13." It was much more than just being an adolescent. Now, it's easy to see that she often felt blue for no apparent reason. She started to confide to my parents that she thought she was depressed. There weren't great resources back then, and they didn't really know how to handle it. I do recall Mom saying, "Oh, Tina, you are just sad sometimes, and that's OK."

Tina felt things more intensely than the rest of us. I was a reasonably happy teenager. Tina was not. I was a pleaser, or "brown noser" as Tina called me. I used to write my mom and dad really nice notes and say things like, "Dear Mom and Dad. I think you are so loving and wonderful, and I am so lucky to be your daughter." Tina would say, "You are such an ass-kisser, and you are so corny." The differences in our dispositions started to create conflict and, sadly, resulted in fighting that lasted a lifetime.

As we grew older, Tina and I had epic physical fights. I liked to invade her space, enter her room when I wanted. She liked her privacy and would tell me to beat it. Clothes were a point of contention, too. If I borrowed something of hers without asking, or vice versa, it would result in fighting. We would pull each other's long hair, throw our wooden clogs at each other, hurl insults until one of us, usually me, would concede. Those battles were short-lived but furious. I could be very mean. We had to walk up our long driveway to meet the school bus. One day, we left for the bus. I don't remember how that fight started, but it escalated as we walked up the driveway. Voices were raised, the heat was up. Finally, I stomped my foot and said, "Just shut up you period woman!" She looked crestfallen and said, "Ingrid, that is so mean." Tina had just started to menstruate, and I knew it was a sensitive topic. I could tell she was really hurt as we boarded the bus, and I knew it was a low blow. I became good at finding her weak spots, and she was good at finding mine.

I have always been an extremely organized person. As a child, my room was rarely messy; it was important to me that it was tidy. Everything had its place. That was one of my weak spots, and Tina knew it. It's actually amazing that I didn't get diagnosed with OCD until my mid-forties.

We had a real blowout when we were in middle school. I can't remember why we started to fight. There was a room off our kitchen that we called the family room. We ate our meals there and did homework at the same table. Tina became so angry with me that she picked up my meticulously organized three-ring binder. "Ingrid, I am going to unclick the rings, turn your binder upside down, and dump all of your schoolwork on the floor." I said, "Tina, don't you dare!" "Just watch me," she replied, and she did exactly what she had promised. When she dropped all the contents on the floor, I screamed at her and hit her, catching the bottom of her right elbow. I didn't know that she was holding a pencil in her right hand. The hand went up toward her face and the pencil tip caught her between her upper lip and the bottom of her nose. She immediately started bleeding, and exclaimed, "Ouch, ouch. The pencil lead is in my face!" She was crying, and I started crying too, and Mom heard us and came running.

"Mom, look at what Ingrid did to my face!" Tina said.

"Mom, she dumped out my binder! I didn't know she was holding a pencil."

Our mom glared at me and said, "Ingrid, look what you've done. I need to take Tina to the doctor right now." They headed to the car. I slumped down to the floor and felt horrible. When they returned a few hours later, Mom said, "Well, Ingrid. The doctor got the pencil lead out, but Tina will always have a scar." She did develop a tiny scar between her nose and her upper lip. Her whole life I looked at that scar and knew that I had caused it.

After elementary school, Tina and I attended different middle schools. When I was in the fifth grade at Three Points Elementary, I informed my parents that I wanted to attend Bush School, a small, nurturing, private school in Seattle. I had listened to my older cousin Ellen Helsell rave about it, especially the drama department, and I had discovered a love for acting. I went through the application process, and while I did, our parents decided if I was going to a private school, then Tina should as well. To them, it seemed only fair.

Tina started at Lakeside School in the seventh grade while I got my dream of being at Bush for sixth grade. Bush was a great decision for me. As a sixth grader, I got to play Juliet in *Romeo and Juliet*. Of course, it's one of the world's greatest love stories. Our acting teacher managed to get us to hold hands just once in the course of the play. That was the best my Romeo (named Matt) and I could do at age twelve. I also loved everything about learning: classes, homework, memorizing, writing papers, organizing my binder. Bush encouraged a love of learning and curiosity. Our class sizes were very small, so we received a lot of individual attention, and I loved that.

I still remember one of my favorite classes in sixth grade: anthropology taught by Mr. Hamilton. Learning about different cultures and artifacts fascinated me. In that class, I met my dear friend Joan, who became a life-long friend. Joan and I went to Bush together and both transferred to Lakeside for high school, where Tina attended. While Tina was at Lakeside and I was at Bush, we took the same bus together into Seattle. The kids who went to Lakeside then transferred to another bus, and we continued on. On the first leg of the bus trip, I met Tina's friend Nancy whom everyone referred to as "Nanny." Nanny is one of the funniest people I know, and she and Tina bonded over their humor. She loved Tina and me and got a kick out of our spicy relationship. She has two sisters herself. When

Nanny boarded the bus, she would look straight at me, wink, and shout out to the entire bus, "Ingrid, you little troublemaker." I would always blush because she pointed me out, but she always made me feel special. When I transferred to Lakeside, Nanny always watched out for me. She was two grades ahead. She went to Stanford ahead of me as well, and we had some mutual friends, including my freshman roommate. Nanny was and is very good friends with Page Hopkins, who turned out to be Tina's best friend in the world.

In the seventh grade, at Lakeside, Tina met Page. They were twelve, both "brace-faced" and in their most awkward teenage phase. I wish that I could insert a video from the mid-70s and show them because describing them together just doesn't do them justice. Picture comedic geniuses Amy Schumer, Kristin Wig, and Maya Rudolph and combine them. Tina and Page had a similar gift for accents and imitations. They created hilarious gestures, poses, and voices which usually resulted in gut-splitting laughter. They amused each other to no end, and often at other people's expenses. They delighted in each other's wit and intelligence. They were both popular girls but edgy enough to never be considered mainstream in their class. They also bonded over the fact that both their mothers were mentally unstable.

After they both started driving, Page used to bomb down our driveway in her mom's red Lincoln Continental, and she always peeled out in the gravel in front of the lawn. Dad used to giggle. "Page must be here," he'd say. One time, she drove over one of Mom's flower beds. Mom was furious. Page is blonde, with gorgeous almond-shaped green eyes and high cheekbones. She has a very distinctive deep voice that served her well in her successful career as a New York City journalist and anchorwoman. I used to love standing outside of Tina's bedroom door, listening to them, and hoping to be invited in. Usually Tina shouted, "Go away Ingrid."

# CHAPTER 4
# High School (1978–1982)

L akeside is a renowned small, private high school in north Seattle. It is a college-preparatory school and considered one of the best private high schools in the nation. Classes were purposefully small and the teachers were interested and interesting. We have a huge family legacy there, starting with our mom's dad. Twenty members of the Clark and Helsell families attended Lakeside. The campus is beautiful and looks like many small eastern college campuses, such as Williams or Amherst. It's a large campus sprinkled with brick buildings, pristine fields and, a big grassy area called the quad where students gather in early fall and late spring to study and socialize. Over the years, there have been many new additions to the school, but its original integrity and beauty remain. After we had all graduated from there, my father was the board president for many years and is now a Trustee Emeritus. Tina and I both loved academia. We were both bright, but she had an intensity for learning that went beyond my capabilities, and I was always jealous of that.

We were both voracious readers. One late night when she was sixteen, she had just finished reading *Jaws*. She climbed into my tiny twin bed with me and said she wasn't leaving. She said, "Ing, I just finished reading *Jaws*, and I am so terrified." I said, "Tina, great white sharks do not live in Lake Washington, nor can they travel up the front lawn and get into our home." There was no persuading her. The fear of the book had grabbed her and she couldn't rid herself of the images. She spent the night snuggled against me. After we had been apart for three years, I joined Tina at Lakeside, my freshman year and her sophomore year.

At Lakeside, I loved the amazing drama department, and I loved my class of one hundred students. On my very first day at Lakeside, I was a little nervous. Midmorning, a beautiful, petite Greek girl named Sophia Solandros Eitel introduced herself to me. It's funny how fate works. Sophia has been my closest friend for forty-three years. Our class of 1982 was an amazingly cohesive and nice group of young people. At reunions, we talk about how there weren't really any cliques and that we were respectful of people's differences. At least that's how I saw it. The class ahead, Tina's class of 1983, was fun, edgier than we were, and maybe not as nice to each other. There were cliques and rivalries. Tina's good friend John used to enjoy putting strange things in my locker; one day between classes, there were whiskers coming through the slats. It was a cat. I have always been a reactor, and people love to tease me to this day. John had pet snakes growing up, and I am terrified of snakes. Hence, the cat seemed like a good option.

Some of the boys in Tina's class would flirt with me. Trust me. Neither Tina nor I were the flirtatious type. I was just more approachable than she was, and I know she didn't like it because I was a new student. I was friendlier than Tina in high school, which caused somewhat of a rift between us. So did the fact that I ended up dating a boy in her class. My first boyfriend, Tony, was in Tina's class. Lakeside has a strong wilderness program. Tony and I ended up on the same three-day camping trip near Mt. Rainier. During the trip, I developed a big crush. I was taken by his dark complexion, chocolate brown eyes, smile, and laugh. We started dating soon after that trip. I remember Tina saying, "I can't believe you like Tony. That is so awkward. He is in my class." After he would visit me at our house, she would ask, "Oh, so were you and Tony making out in your room?" Tina did not have a crush on Tony, but she didn't like it that I was dating him, and that made it awkward. Plus, our dad always thought it was funny to give our boyfriends a nickname. Tony's was "Antonius Dwyeris." Tony was a trooper for putting up with me and Tina, and a wonderful first boyfriend. At Tina's memorial, he hugged me and said, "Ingrid, I spent a lot of time at your house."

Our friend Jessica also spent a lot of time at our home. Without a doubt Jessica was the one friend Tina and I happily shared growing up. Jessica was my age and in my class at Lakeside, but she was mature and loved hanging out with older kids. Jessica was fun. She was energetic and whimsical. She was the kind of person you wanted to be around. She had two sisters, so she understood girls. She loved clothes, and Tina and I used to covet her impressive sweater collection. Jessica and Tina appreciated each other's humor and the fact that they could both be a little naughty at times. Tina's humor often verged a little on the raunchy side, and she gave Jess a curious nickname, Yuicy, which seemed to fit her. Jessica was the one friend who could come over and roam between Tina's room and my room, with little animosity between Tina and me. I think it's because we shared different things. While Jessica and I bonded over being the same age and having similar interests, she and Tina bonded over liking older kids and being a little on the fringe. When Alexa was born, Jessica, Tina, and I went to the hospital to meet our baby sister for the first time, born on Tina's seventeenth birthday.

I played the piano growing up. I was never that great, and my hands are very small, so I could never reach an octave. Jess used to watch and listen to me play the piano. When I was sixteen, she sat down at our piano and played Beethoven's "Fur Elise." I watched her dumbfounded. I asked, "Jessica, how in the world do you know how to play that?" She said, "I've been listening to you play that for months." Immediately I found Mom in her bedroom and said, "I am never taking another piano lesson again. Jessica just played 'Fur Elise' because she listened to it. She has a natural ear." Mom didn't argue.

Our senior year, Jessica and I were the leads in the musical *The Boyfriend*. Turns out her natural ear lent itself to an incredible singing voice. As an adult, Jessica continued to perform in various shows and performances. In December of 2019, Jessica sang Christmas songs at an event in Seattle. She sang so beautifully that I teared up the entire performance. Watching her sing made me miss Tina and the times the three of us were together. I wanted Tina beside me to celebrate our friend.

I would be remiss in describing our high school years without talking about our carpool. My parents had a big blue car called a Travellall, made by International Harvester. It was the forerunner of our modern-day SUVs. Before Tina and I got our driver's licenses, my parents had John Hoedemaker drive us to Lakeside. Page and Jessica have helped me fill in the details of this funny squad. It was John and four girls, Tina, me, Jessica, and Page. He would pick up Jessica and Page at the entrance to the 520 floating bridge and then come get Tina and me. John decided to name the car Eda because the license plate began with EDA. As John describes it, "She was a lumbering old beast, took full throttle and patience to get her up to freeway speed—no headrests and maybe no seatbelts?" John also reminded me of the gas crisis in the 1970s and that Eda got about three miles per gallon. The beast had an eight-track cassette player. We drove the twenty-five minutes to Lakeside listening to The Cars ("Bye Love"), the Rolling Stones ("Shattered," "Beast of Burden"), George Thorogood ("Bad to the Bone") Van Halen ("Ain't Talking 'Bout Love"), and even Leif Garrett ("I Was Made for Dancing"). Jessica and I were madly in love with Leif.

After Tina got her license, she would drive us to Lakeside until the end of her junior year when we finally got our licenses. Jess loved to ride shotgun, so she could DJ and play music for us. It annoyed me that she always wanted the front seat, but it helped that her musical selections were consistently good. One summer, we begged Tina to drive us to the Puyallup Fair to hear Leif Garrett sing. She did. While we were at his concert, there was a young woman, very pregnant, crying and holding up a flip chart with requests like "Leif, please marry me." Watching her made me sad. She was too young to be pregnant, and she was infatuated with a teen idol who would never be interested in her. As a result, I very quickly lost interest in Leif. On the drive home, Tina made fun of me and Jess, saying how dumb we were to like him. Regardless, the carpool was hilarious. It was a carload full of laughter, songs, gossip, and general teenage angst. Linda Hoedemaker told me how glad she was that she went to a different high school. She said our carpool would have been too much for her. Bless John Hodie for putting up with us!

In the spring of her junior year, Tina decided she wanted to go abroad. I believe the situation with leaving Lakeside for one quarter required her to submit a research project. She decided she wanted to study the French painter Henri Marie Raymond de Toulouse Lautrec. He was probably best known for his painting "At the Moulin Rouge" (1890). She went to Albi in southern France, northeast of the city of Toulouse. She lived with a French family with two boys and a girl. Tina shared a room with Bebe (pronounced Beebee). Bebe had a boyfriend, chain-smoked, and wore her jeans so tight that she had to lie down on her bed to pull them on. One time I remember Tina calling home, and in the background, a boy was being loud. She said, "*Tais-toi, Frank. Je parle avec mes parents aux Etats-Unis.*" (Be quiet Frank. I am speaking with my parents in the United States.) Mom was so tickled that she was speaking French. Tina told me that at one of her first family dinners, the mother asked her if she wanted more to eat. She said, "*No merci. Je suis plein.*" Although "plein" means full in French, most French interpret that phrase as "I am pregnant." She should have said, "*No, merci, j'ai assez mange,*" which means "I have eaten enough." Apparently, the family had a good chuckle over her response. I was so in awe of her flying abroad and living in a different country. I also vividly remember her calling home on May 18, 1980, the day Mount St. Helens erupted. She was worried about us.

When Tina left for France, our sister Alexa was just three months old. Alexa's arrival into our family changed everything. She brought us so much joy, life, and preciousness. Alexa was born on January 16, 1981, sharing a birthday with Tina, seventeen years apart. I'll never forget when my parents announced that she was on the way. Dad had taken Tina, me, and another father-daughter duo on a college tour back East. When we returned home, our parents sat us down in the family room. Dad said, "Kids, your mother and I have something to tell you. Your mom is pregnant." I was sixteen and kind of grossed out; it meant I had to envision our parents having sex. Also, my mom was forty. It was 1980. All of their best friends had their children in their early 20s, and they were all about to become empty nesters. They explained that Mom was either going to get a full-time job or continue to be a stay-at-home mom and have another child.

Now I wonder if Dad knew Mom was really unstable and thought another child would be a good diversion for her. In retrospect, she absolutely should have tried to find a full-time job instead. However, Alexa is the best thing that ever happened to our family. I tell everyone that Mom and Dad got it perfectly right with Alexa. She is smart, creative, hardworking, kind, tall, and gorgeous.

Alexa's arrival also signified the beginning of our mom's downward spiral into depression, the abuse of drugs and alcohol, and general disintegration as a mom and human being. After she delivered Alexa at age forty, her life took a downward turn that she never recovered from. At this point, Tina was seventeen, I was sixteen, and Spencer was twelve. We were at tender times in our lives when we really needed her, but she wasn't there, at least not emotionally.

Tina graduated in 1981 from Lakeside, and I in 1982. She opted to follow our dad's footsteps and chose Dartmouth College. I stayed on the west coast and went to Stanford. When Tina returned from her freshman fall at Dartmouth, her first visitor was Jessica. They hugged and raced out to the car. They played Ricky Lee Jones' *Pirate* cassette, singing along at the top of their lungs, "We Belong Together."

# CHAPTER 5

# Linda Clark Helsell

To understand Tina's pathology, one must understand our mom and her history of mental illness. Her instability, anger, and unhealthy relationship with Tina affected Tina in a powerfully tragic way. Linda Mary Clark was born to Spencer and Myra Clark in Calgary, Alberta, in 1941. The family moved from Canada to the US when she was three. She was the oldest of four children.

Because of our grandmother's hearing and anger issues, it's safe to say that our mother had a very weak role model. Mom carried the rage and insecurity of her childhood into our lives. I have always wondered why she and my father decided to have four children because she did not have the emotional tools or patience a mother needs to have. She was as beautiful as her mother, but in a different way. She was brunette with brown eyes, red lips, and a pretty, curvy figure. My memories of her from early childhood are very special. She was a hard worker, an avid gardener, a nurturer, and an athlete. She was a great skier and tennis player. She did a lot of development work in Seattle in the 70s, before development positions were paid. She was active with the YWCA, the magazine *Puget Soundings*, and many other organizations. She was the consummate volunteer.

Mom was much closer to her dad—our grandfather—than she was to her mom. He died four months before Alexa was born. At that point, he was displaying incredible mania. He had been hospitalized for an ulcer, but his death resulted from a fall in the hospital and a head injury. He was only sixty-five. Now that I am fifty-seven, that seems so young. I remember when we got the phone call that he had died. My room was closest to my parents, and I could hear Mom wailing in the early hours of the morning. He had an ulcer. He wasn't supposed to die. Because of postpartum depression and his death, Mom went down a path of depression and unpredictable behavior. She started seeing a psychiatrist whose method was invasive childhood work. Instead of moving forward, he made her dive deep into her childhood. He had come highly recommended from one of her friends. I was only seventeen, but even then, I knew none of this methodology was helpful.

Mom had gained a lot of weight during her pregnancy. After Alexa was born, this same psychiatrist put her on a diet, consisting of diet coke and sandwich meats. All protein, no carbs, and I don't recall any veggies. That is all she consumed for months. She had a complicated relationship with food. She hated cooking, and her meals were terrible. One night at dinner, Spence said, "Mom, all we ever eat is chicken, chili, fish. Chicken, chili, fish! Can we have something different?" She rarely sat down at the dinner table with us, but when she was doing the dishes, she ate everyone's leftovers.

Mom developed an obsession with weight, and especially her daughters' weights. I was built smaller than Tina, or different. I have my mom's figure: big breasts, smaller lower half, curvy. Tina was a true natural beauty and received a lot of attention for her looks. She had large, wide-set brown eyes, high cheek bones, and lustrous thick, long dark hair. She was small-busted and small-waisted but had large thighs. She inherited our dad's legs. Instead of Mom making her proud of her physique, she body-shamed her. At some point in high school, Tina got caught for shoplifting laxatives from the local pharmacy. When she was seventeen, Tina went on the Scarsdale diet, which is essentially a starvation diet. I joined her because our soccer coach told our whole team we needed to lose weight. I lost ten pounds and Tina lost thirty. She received a lot of attention for getting so thin but sadly, mostly from our mom. Mom also used to sneak into Tina's room and try on her clothes, determined not to outweigh or outsize her oldest daughter.

Mom taught us to equate our self-worth with how we looked. She constantly talked about other people's weight. She damaged Tina and me in that way. I know it was Mom's mental illness that made her so cruel, but it still feels unforgiveable. It's hard enough being a woman in the US without having a mother who is obsessive about body types. I feel fortunate that I've never had an eating disorder, which, given the circumstances, seems like a small miracle. I do think about my figure and weight more than I want to.

In addition to being obsessed with weight, our mom entered a truly ugly phase of wanting anything and everything associated with a high social status. She became enamored of fancy cars, designer clothes, knowing all the right people, knowing the wealthiest people. She started drinking too much. We had an army of people working for us because she couldn't handle the day-to-day. Alexa had a full-time nanny named Lorraine. In addition to Lorraine, there was a young beautiful yogi named Vera who helped drive Alexa places and did chores. We had Elizabeth, who cleaned our home for twenty years, and a cook named David, who prepared meals once a week and froze them for us. At some point in high school, David came to me and told me Mom wanted him to get her drugs—weed, cocaine. So, not only were we living with her instability, bad temper, and body-shaming, but we also had to start dealing with her addictions.

Here are some typical scenes from that time:

- Ingrid, preparing to go to college with no help from her mom. Mom is lying in her bed, watching movies, eating chocolates. Mom yells at Ingrid, says, "You are spoiled rotten" because Ingrid shows her a $25 shirt she purchased.

- Young Spencer and his best friend Stephen finding Linda asleep on her toilet, numerous times. Too much booze and/or pills.

- On a family vacation, Mom yelling at fifteen-year-old Alexa in a crowded restaurant because Alexa doesn't want to talk about a rape scene from a book. My mom became fascinated by tragic events and liked to discuss them, often at inappropriate times.

- Quivering eleven-year-old Ingrid listening to her parents scream and yell at each other as her mother dumps all of her father's neatly appointed work files out the second story window of their home. They were having a terrible fight, and my mom knew the best way to hurt my organized father was to make a mess of his paperwork.

- Sitting through dinners with Mom's new friends from down the street. He was a wealthy ophthalmologist from the South and his wife, a beautiful German heiress. He was an incredible racist. He would use the N word at our dinner table. I was in my teens and absolutely dumbfounded at my mother's insatiable need to know wealthy people, even if they were the most horrible human beings. After two meals with that couple, I told Mom that I would not attend another meal with them. I never really understood how Dad coped with it. He is a very decent man, and I know he didn't really like this couple. The dynamics in our family were so confusing.

- One night in high school, I was sitting in our hot tub with my friend Peter from high school. Mom came out on the balcony above us and started talking to us, about the evening, school. She had a glass of chardonnay in her hand and was wearing a completely see-through nightgown, all body parts visible. It seemed like she stayed there forever. I didn't understand at the time that exhibitionism was part of her illness.

These are but a few of the scenes we witnessed growing up. Anyone reading this book who had or currently has a parent who suffers from mental illness and addiction knows the fear and instability it brings. There was yelling and abusive language. Mom's temper was quick to ignite and slow to dissipate. Whenever our family left a party or gathering together, Mom used to say unkind things about people, like, "She has gained so much weight," or "That woman has always been such a bitch." There was so much negative talk. Mom used to boast about how good she was at writing bereavement notes. Bereavement notes are an acknowledgment of someone's pain. I used to love being at my friends' homes, listening to their gentle mothers ask me questions about my life. Their moms weren't weight-obsessed or addicted to alcohol and pills.

Despite all of this, there were good moments with our mom. She did love us, and I suppose she did the best job she could with the tools she had. While I was researching this book and speaking with many childhood friends, they always told me they loved my mom. I am glad she was able to show her good side to them. But for Tina and me, we often felt like we were living a lie because our closest friends didn't really witness our mom's unpredictable moods and anger.

We were fortunate to have a stable, mentally healthy father. However, he enabled my mom to act badly, and he travelled a lot for his work while we were growing up. She was so difficult that we all tiptoed around her, much like she did around her mom when she was younger. She was too much for any of us to handle. This was especially true for Tina. She was the eldest and was expected to assume more responsibility than me, Spencer and, of course, our baby Alexa. Mom was harder on Tina for everything. It took an emotional toll on Tina that affected her the rest of her life.

Tina's relationship with Mom was ill-fated from the start. My parents were married when Mom was twenty-one and Dad, twenty-four. Mom was all set to start teaching history at Queen Anne High School in Seattle, but she soon discovered that she was pregnant with Tina. I don't know the exact timing of this, but the story is that my mom was really sad about getting pregnant so soon, and somehow it interrupted her ability to teach.

I firmly believe if a woman is depressed during pregnancy, it has to affect the baby in utero. One of Tina's dear friends, Catherine Monk, is a psychologist at Columbia University. Her focus is on women's health during pregnancy. Her team is doing cutting-edge work about women who suffer from depression and how it affects the fetus. They are doing preventive work to ensure that both mom and baby are taken care of in the best possible way. Catherine and I talk frequently about her work, as it pertains to her friend and my sister.

When Tina was old enough to understand, Mom told her that she wasn't excited to have her at the time, that she wasn't ready. Again, I know it was mental illness, but I am certain Mom never needed to share that. Mom and Tina struggled because Tina challenged her. Tina wasn't easy, but she wasn't difficult either. Either Mom didn't appreciate all the wonderful qualities Tina had, or maybe she was jealous of her humor, her beauty, but mostly her intelligence. Whichever it was, Mom wasn't thrilled to find herself pregnant with Tina and never seemed to get over her resentment of her. When I came along, there was no resentment. I was also born June 6, but my day of arrival was supposed to be the end of August. I weighed three pounds, four ounces at birth, and spent the first month of my life in an incubator. My beginning was tenuous, and I was never a threat to a career path. To this day, I have guilt about having postpartum depression with our oldest son Henry. I hope it didn't carry over to him, but how can I be certain? I was happy during the pregnancy, albeit very sick the first fourteen weeks.

It's safe to say Tina spent her entire life despising our mom. She never felt fully loved or accepted by her. When Tina took her life, Mom was already deep into dementia. At Tina's memorial, I sat next to my parents, but I don't think Mom really understood what was happening. Had it happened several years earlier, she would have known and it would have devastated her. In the years before the dementia crept in, she had tried to repair their relationship. But by then, Tina's illness had escalated. It was too late and too much harm had been done. I am grateful that Mom didn't really understand Tina's death because I couldn't have handled her intense grief coupled with my own.

Tina had to assume more than most children because our mom was incapable of truly being the adult. I remember this one painful incident when we were in high school. Mom had asked Tina if she could drive her to her doctor's appointment. She had her monthly checkup with her OB, and she must have been about six months pregnant. Tina said she couldn't because she had to finish a paper for school. Mom became irrational and started yelling at Tina. Mom stormed out of the house. She had left her passenger door open and forgot to close it. She drove out of the garage and the door ripped off. It was so frightening and emotional and a burden Tina should not have had at seventeen. Tina wasn't completely "parentalized," but it was close.

Tina never really took an interest in being with the whole family. We would spend one week every summer up in British Columbia, on *Bohemia*. One on trip, we were anchored in a beautiful spot called Walsh Cove. My parents had probably shared a bottle or two of chardonnay at dinner, and their snoring was epic. Our boat wasn't very big. Tina and I eventually moved from our bunks to the cockpit. We could still hear the snoring, and it was driving Tina nuts. She said, "Ing, I am going to row ashore and sleep on that little island." I said, "You can't do that. What if there are animals?" She said, "I don't care. That snoring is driving me mad." She did go toward the stern where the dingy was tied, but decided against rowing ashore. We eventually fell asleep in the cockpit, both holding pillows over our ears. When Tina was about seventeen, she stopped joining us in Canada and would stay at a friend's house.

This past August, I was in our garden pruning my roses and listening to the podcast *Dear Therapists* with Lori Gottlieb and Guy Winch. These amazing therapists were interviewing a Korean woman named Molly. Molly and her family had moved to the US from Korea when she was very young. She became everything to her parents, their interpreter, their link to society, their driver, their lifeline. Lori and Guy called this a situation when a child becomes "parentalized" at a young age; essentially, they lose their childhood to assume adult responsibilities. When Molly was a grown woman, her father took his life. Her mother eventually told Molly it was her fault. Her mother was so devastated that she had to blame his death on somebody. To hear Molly cry and hear the pain in her voice made me crumble. Of course, her father's suicide wasn't Molly's fault. Molly's pain reminded me of Tina's.

Because of how Mom treated Tina and sometimes me, I couldn't love or treasure my twenty-year-old daughter, Hazel, more than I do. Our upbringing taught me that the relationship between mother and daughter is crucial. A mom should emulate strength, compassion, and courage. When she was little, I used to say, "Hazel, you should always be the nice girl." Now I realize I should have said, "Hazel, you must have your own voice in this world." Hazel and I have definitely had our trying periods; high school was no picnic. She is in college now. I have watched her grow into a mature young woman, a student, a friend, a girlfriend, and a humanitarian.

CHAPTER 6

# Mom's Fall

When my mom turned sixty, she went to the renowned Hazelden clinic outside of Portland, Oregon, to treat her addictions to alcohol and pain medications. Several weeks into her treatment, she fell into such a deep depression that she had to be flown to the psychiatric ward at Northwest Hospital in Seattle. At this point, she had been diagnosed as bipolar. Tina, Alexa, and I went to visit her one day. When we walked into her room, she was on her bed, and Dad was in a nearby chair reading the newspaper. When she saw the three of us, she smiled. Dad said, "That is the first smile I have seen in days." There was a little Buddha on her bedside table. Tina said, "Oh, Mom has the Buddha I gave her."

Mom's psychiatrist met with us in a private room. He explained, "This is a difficult situation with your mom. We have to be really careful with her medications; we want to lift her out of this deep depression without throwing her into a manic state." I remember Alexa and I being very teary at that meeting, while Tina was dry-eyed and calm. At that moment, I knew Tina felt no real attachment to Mom, even though she was in the depths of her illness. It surprised me, given that Tina suffered from depression as well. Eventually, Mom was stabilized, and then she had to return to Hazelden to finish her treatment. That experience was the turning point for me as her daughter, now a grown woman and a mother. I realized just how hard her life had been. Her mental illness dominated her. My anger turned toward compassion, which must have been a relief to Eric. I'd spent the first ten years of our marriage being really, really angry with her.

Today Mom is 81. She has been in a group home for six years with dementia. She is heavy now because she just sits all day long. She uses a walker, and she has to wear diapers. She recognizes me but doesn't know my name. On one visit, Alexa, Spencer, and I went together. She turned to me, pointed at them and asked, "Are they in love?" She introduces me as "her friend." She has no short or long-term memory. I ache for her now because she has no life. Despite all of it, I still love my mom. I also know that her dementia is likely a direct result of years of addiction, drug abuse, and mental illness.

We were fortunate to be fairly affluent growing up, but if I had to live my childhood over again, I would rather have a smaller home, less money, and a normal mother. I firmly believe that our mom's mental illness and behaviors shaped the four of us, and we have all had mental health struggles, though Tina's was the most severe. Money, status, and privilege became everything to our mom, but they didn't bring her joy or lead her to a productive life. We did have money, thanks to a very hard-working and wonderful father. Robert Morton Helsell is the next piece of the fabric of Tina's life.

# CHAPTER 7

# Robert Morton Helsell

My father might be one of the most loved men in the city of Seattle. He is smart, kind, funny, and has a huge smile for everyone. Robert Morton Helsell was born in 1937, the youngest of four siblings, son of Frank and Ellen Helsell. He was the baby by thirteen years. Both his brothers, Jack and Bill, fought in WW2. Jack was a member of the 10th Mountain Division and later the US infantry. Bill was a naval aviator and flew off carriers. Dad also had a sister named Ruth. Ruth was married and had three children but later in her life fell in love with a woman, got divorced, and moved to England, where her partner lived. Dad is eighty-four, and the only living member of his family today.

Dad received his BS in Engineering and an MBE (Master of Business Engineering) at Dartmouth College. He started his career as an engineer, then became a CPA, and later moved into the construction industry, where he spent most of his career. Eventually he achieved his professional dream of owning his own construction company, Wilder Construction. He experienced a lot of joy while he was running Wilder. He met and fell in love with Mom when she was at Skidmore College on the East Coast, even though they were both from the Seattle area. She spent one year at Skidmore, one year studying abroad in Geneva, and then finished her college degree at the University of Washington.

Our father travelled a lot when we were growing up. His business took him mostly to Alaska and Texas. Consequently, I don't think he ever really had the full picture of our mom's instability as a parent. I think she did a great job of faking it and covering up. My only complaint about him as a father is that even though we would often go to him and try to tell him how frightening Mom's temper was, he always stood by her. Perhaps he had to because he was away so much. By the time Alexa was born, his career was established, and he spent a lot of time with her. I think Alexa actually saved him from dealing with Mom. Dad and Alexa have a very special relationship, one that I am perhaps a wee bit jealous of.

Our mom also had a very manipulative way of using Dad as a scapegoat. She would say things like, "Ingrid, your father will be very disappointed if you make that decision." It was always untrue. Ninety percent of the time she had never even discussed the situation with him, but she was able to control us that way because we didn't want to disappoint Dad.

Every single night Dad came home from work, he entered through the screen door by the kitchen and whistled to alert us to his presence. I always welcomed and loved that whistle because it meant the stable parent was home. That whistle represented safety. As a child, I wrote in a journal, and I have kept a few of them. In one journal entry dated Sept. 13, 1982, I wrote, "Sometimes I think Dad is my savior. He always comes home cheery and wonderfully interested in our days. Mom is enough to make me cry."

Dad added love and stability to our lives, which is why I think we all turned out OK. He was an incredibly hard worker and took his job as the family provider very seriously. In some ways, my husband Eric is like him; Eric works harder than anyone I know. He treasures the four of us and his extended family and always prioritizes us when making big decisions.

Tina and Dad had a very special relationship. They shared a love for family, education, and humor. Their intelligence bonded them, as did their hard work ethic. She was his firstborn, and I know from experience that is a unique bond. My favorite story about Dad and Tina involves her trip to Taiwan one summer to attend an immersive Mandarin speaking course. This was circa 1984. We didn't have cell phones. Tina flew from Seattle to Los Angeles for her leg to Taipei. While waiting for her flight, she decided she wanted to phone a few of her friends to say goodbye. In order to do this, she had to have the operator call our home number and get permission from my dad to place a long-distance call. Dad knew exactly when Tina's plane was departing. For the first phone call, Dad agreed. The second time the operator called, Dad agreed but knew her flight was boarding soon. When the operator called a third time, he said, "Tell my daughter to get on the goddamned plane!" About fifteen minutes later, Tina called home, sobbing to Dad, "Dad, I missed my flight." Dad was furious.

For years, they laughed about that story. Of course, Dad's version was different than Tina's. Just as it was for me, it was hard for him when she became ill because she had changed so much. Toward the end of her life, she became very reliant on him. I know she felt ashamed of her dependency because as the oldest child, she had always been the strong one.

About ten years ago, my father admitted to Tina that he had wanted to divorce Mom when Tina and I were two and three years old. He knew that she was not stable. As he told me recently, "Your mother was a chronic liar." One day, he was driving across the 520 bridge that connects Seattle to the city of Bellevue. He got caught in traffic, and while he was waiting, he told himself that it was time to divorce Linda. He was exhausted by her bad behavior and her lies. When he pulled into our driveway, he saw Tina and me riding our big wheels in the backyard, and we were giggling. He couldn't bear the thought of leaving us, possibly solely in her care, so he stayed in the marriage through many, many difficult years. He is a very kind, traditional man. As he told me many times, "Ingrid, I honored my wedding vows."

Dad is now happily involved with a lovely woman named Patsy who lost her husband in a tragic accident five years ago. She is also eighty-four and a ninety-pound ball of energy. She is loving, a tremendous cook, gardener, mother, and grandmother. Dad smiles all the time because I think he finally knows what having a true partner is all about. And he so deserves it. I am grateful he can experience this, even in the twilight of his life.

# CHAPTER 8
# College (1981–1986)

The day Tina left for Dartmouth was one of the saddest days of my life. When Tina left, I felt like half of me was gone. She left a note on my bed, along with some sisterly treasures: "These are for you. I love you." They were some of my favorite clothes of hers. I sat on my bed, held the sweaters that had her scent, and sobbed. I was sad not only that she had left but also because I had to face Mom and all of her issues without Tina. That's when Tina and I started to get really close, the day she left for college. Even though we often fought, when she left for Dartmouth, I missed her intensely. I missed her laugh, her jokes, her beautiful face, her smell. She always smelled good.

After Page left Lakeside for Madeira, Tina's friend Catherine Monk also left to attend Andover on the east coast. At Andover, Catherine made a really good friend: Sally Schwartz from Chicago. Sally was headed to Dartmouth, and Catherine told her that she must meet Tina Helsell. Sally ended up becoming one of Tina's dearest friends. In Sally's words, "When I met Tina for the first time, she was carrying an African woven bag with a leather strap, and her gorgeous hair reached her underwear line. She was a Bohemian beauty, and I had an instant girl crush." Tina had a close group of about five women from different parts of the country. Sally describes their posse as the anti-jock, counterculture group of young women. They were popular but a little on the fringe, similar to how Tina and Page were in high school. At that time, Dartmouth offered a winter term off for students to pursue internships. Tina and Sally decided to spend their sophomore winter in New York City.

Sally and Tina shared a two-bedroom apartment together, at 72 Barrow St. in the Village. Sally had an internship at Conde Nast and Tina at Art in America. Looking back at that time Sally remembers Tina spending a lot of time asleep in her futon. Sally would leave in the mornings with Tina curled up under her covers, and often when she returned, Tina would still be in bed. Somedays Tina just wouldn't go to her internship. Sally realizes now it was Tina's clinical depression that kept her in bed. They did go out at night and party with friends, but the stay-at-home pattern was there, and it wasn't normal.

I wasn't accepted at Williams College, the school I had my heart set on, but I was accepted at Stanford. Stanford in the 1980s wasn't nearly as competitive as it is today. Nevertheless, Mom became obsessed with my attending Stanford because it meant status. It had almost nothing to do with whether or not I wanted to attend. Ironically, years later, in one of Mom's moods, she raised her voice at me and said, "Ingrid, you should have never gone to Stanford! You should have studied drama at a small, liberal arts college." Then she left the family room and slammed the door on her way out. I wasn't sure it was the right school for me. I was dumfounded by the competition I was up against. I was also intrigued by the number of boarding school kids from the East Coast who just jumped into college; they had already been away from home for four years. They were independent and wonderfully confident.

Back then, far more local kids were being accepted. Stanford to the Bay Area was more like the University of Washington is to the Seattle region. Stanford honored many of the promising locals with a letter of acceptance. One of these students was my wonderful freshman roommate, Antonia Moore. We are very different people, but we became the best of friends our freshman year and have remained so ever since. We share a love of humanity and goodness and have the kind of friendship that is based on true respect for each other.

Fast forward a year. I was starting my sophomore fall at Stanford, had made some great friends, and enjoyed being there. The professors, the beautiful campus, northern California sunshine, and proximity to

San Francisco and local beaches were also a plus. I started to feel proud of myself for doing well academically at Stanford. And then, everything changed. That same fall, Tina decided to transfer from Dartmouth to Stanford to major in East Asian studies. The East Asian Studies Department at Stanford was excellent, and Tina wanted to trade the bitterly cold New Hampshire winters for California sun. She had spent the previous summer on the Stanford campus enrolled in an intensive Mandarin course, and she loved it. She wanted to become fluent in Mandarin.

To this day, I regret feeling this way, but I resented her for joining me there. It was a love/hate situation from the start. We loved each other so much, and I was grateful she wasn't three thousand miles away anymore. However, she was never as good at making friends as I was, so she mostly joined my friend group. We had a Diesel Dasher car that we shared. We were supposed to take turns having the car at college each year, but because she lived off campus, she needed the car to get to and from campus. We spent a lot of time together, but we also had several terrible fights, one of which all my roommates witnessed my senior year. But mostly, I wanted out of her academic shadow. We were both bright, but she had an intensity for learning that was unparalleled. She learned how to read, speak, and write Mandarin by the time she was twenty-five, between Stanford and intensive summers at a language school in Taiwan. I was more of a generalist, and I was jealous of her superior academic abilities.

Our social lives became too intertwined. Fairly soon after Tina arrived on the Stanford scene, she met and fell in love with Pierre. Born and raised in Boston, Pierre was French-American and, quite simply, gorgeous. He was also charming, smart, artsy, and spoke English and French fluently. Pierre was very good friends with my boyfriend John. Tina also befriended Hilary, a good friend of both mine and John's. Hilary was a magnetic, compassionate, and captivating woman. People would literally line up at the Stanford coffee house to talk to Hilary. She was brutally honest, funny, and an incredible conversationalist. Both Pierre and Hilary had attended East Coast boarding schools; they were savvy and always interested in meeting new people. I had a girl crush on Hilary, as did many others. Hilary and Tina became really good friends and spent a lot of time together. I was jealous of that too. I wanted Hilary to be my friend, not our friend.

When I was a senior and Tina was in her fifth-year master's program, we both developed a crush on the same guy. One afternoon after our classes, Tina and I met up on a bench outside of Tressider, Stanford's student union building. I was so excited to tell her about my crush. I said, "Tina, I have the biggest crush on Mark. He is so cute and so nice, and I think he kind of likes me too." Tina looked like I had stabbed her in the heart. She said, "Are you kidding me? I have the biggest crush on Mark, and I have for weeks." We were both completely silent for a few minutes. Then I said, "What are we going to do? I really like him." "Well, I really like him too," she responded.

I was so angry at that moment that I wanted to yell, "You came to my college, you drive the car I was supposed to drive, you come to my room and borrow my clothes without asking, your closest friends are my closest friends, your grade point is higher than mine, and now you like the same guy I do?!" I did not say any of that to her.

Mark and I did go out on a few dates; there was a little spark, but I couldn't commit to seeing where the relationship would go because I didn't want to hurt Tina. In the end, my loyalty and love were always to Tina. My relationship with her was more important than trying to see where a relationship with Mark would go, especially since we were about to leave. We graduated the same day because she stayed an extra year for her master's degree. She graduated with honors.

After the ceremony, Mom said, "Ingrid, I noticed in the program that Tina and several of your friends graduated with honors, but you did not." So, getting accepted to and graduating from Stanford was still not good enough. I was supposed to graduate with honors. The morning after we graduated, we met our father for brunch in San Francisco. At that brunch, he told Tina she should use her Mandarin and go to work for the Lindblad travel company, leading tours in China. Then he turned to me and said, "Ingrid, I think you should be a stewardess. You can work your way up. Airlines are a great industry." This is absolutely no slight against flight attendants. I have friends who are flight attendants, and they are intelligent, capable people. However, I felt like he was saying, "Tina is smarter than you because she speaks Mandarin." If Tina hadn't joined me at Stanford, it could have been what I wanted it to be: my own experience away from my family. I made the mistake of pointing that out to Tina a few months before she took her life. She did not appreciate my sentiment. I feel terrible that I told her, but I can't apologize because she is dead.

# CHAPTER 9

# The Infamous Trip to Japan and China (Summer of 1985)

As a precursor to Tina's career, our parents decided to take us to China; it was the summer before my senior year, and her fifth year at Stanford. Since we were traveling all the way to Asia, they thought we should stop in Japan first. Alexa was only five, so she stayed at home with her nanny while we traveled to Japan and China. The five of us flew from Seattle to Tokyo. I haven't been back to Japan since I was twenty-one, but travelling around Japan back then was very tricky, as there are absolutely no signs or directions in English. (Not that there should be, but we were unprepared) Tokyo is crowded, colorful, and fascinating, but I felt like we had landed on a different planet. It was hot. We never knew what to order in the restaurants or how to do it. One night, I accidentally ordered a really good beef noodle soup, and my family looked on with envy as they tried to eat what they ordered.

One day, we took the bullet train from Tokyo to Kyoto. The gardens and temples in Kyoto were very beautiful. Dad reminded me that he had left our passports in Tokyo, so we weren't admitted to the best museums in Kyoto. He was already on edge. Tina, Spencer, and I were also out of sorts. Spencer spent the train ride to and from Kyoto, sitting behind Tina and me, pulling our long hair. By the time we returned to Tokyo, the three of us were fighting badly. Our dad said, "If you three are going to continue like this, your mother and I are going to China and you can go home." In our minds, the three of us wanted to respond, "Yes please. Send us home."

This was China in 1985. It wasn't easy traveling. The government collected our passports at the beginning of our trip and only returned them on our departure to Hong Kong. Some of the hotel rooms were downright creepy, laden with heavy red drapes, and uncomfortable stiff sheets. The airplane trips between major cities were frightening. The planes were old and the seats, rickety. Spencer was cracking up on one flight. The flight attendants were practically throwing little packages of gray meats to passengers. We were all out of our comfort zone.

Dad had decided that since Tina spoke Mandarin, he wouldn't need to hire a tour guide in China. We had drivers in each city and some local assistance, but Tina was meant to lead us. Talk about pressure on Tina. At the beginning of the trip, Tina was asked if we wanted "low," "medium," or "high" level food during the two-week excursion. Of course, she chose "high." As it turns out, "high" level food was what the Empresses ate in the earlier dynasties. I'm talking gelatinous fish, quivering eyeballs, unidentifiable meats. We hardly ate, and I am sure the Chinese were offended. We kept seeing large tour groups seated, eating delectable bowls of steaming rice and noodles with prawns. At one point in the journey, Mom completely embarrassed us by trying to pantomime eating a bowl of noodles. Then she said out loud, "Noodles. We want noodles!" We couldn't change the level of food once we started because the decision was made in Beijing where we started, and there wasn't flexibility along the way. Also, the temperature was in the 80s on the streets, but there was only lukewarm Orange Fanta, Coke, and water to drink. I could never quench my thirst.

Our first driver in Beijing was a very nice man named Mr. Wang. His English was passable, but funny. He would say things like, "Please to prepare your umbrellas to get off the car." He had a picture of his wife hanging from his rearview mirror. Mom said, "Mr. Wang, your wife is very beautiful." He replied, "She's not beautiful but she's not bad." That is still one of my favorite lines. Tensions grew high among us. By the time we arrived in the southern city Suchow, everyone was crabby, hot, and hungry. I had left an envelope with my traveler's checks on the train to Suchow. Fortunately, I had the receipt saved in another bag, but I begged everyone not to tell Dad. Somehow, he found out, and he was angry. He asked Tina to try to find an American Express office. Eventually, we did locate one, but the sign reading "American Express" was dangling off its hooks and nobody could help Tina.

We specifically went to Suchow, so Mom could see the famous gardens. In the middle of a very crowded side street full of Chinese on their bicycles, Dad yelled, "Linda, you can take these Suchow gardens and shove them up your ass!" Nice. The gardens were subpar, to say the least. Later that night, our dad was so glum that Spencer and I went in search of something that might make him happy. There was a bar on one of the upper floors, and we bought him a bottle of scotch and a jar of Planters peanuts and brought them to his room. "Here, Dad. These are for you," said Spence. Dad grumbled, "I am not hungry."

Later Mom came down the staircase in an Yves Saint Laurent polka-dotted pantsuit, and our local guide said, "Mrs. Helsell, you look very shiny tonight." To which she replied, "Well, thank you. This is an Yves Saint Laurent." The absurdity of that alone still makes me giggle, that a man in rural China would have any idea who Yves St. Laurent was. She had to display her status wherever we were. One of our last cities before Hong Kong was the southern city of Nanjing. We stayed in a very nice hotel there, and we were so excited that we could get ice cream sundaes for dessert. Tina had brought a Jane Fonda workout tape with her, and when we could, she and I would exercise along with Jane in the hotel room. Spencer's teasing hadn't ended with the hair-pulling on the bullet train. He would often enter the room while we were working out and mimic us and the exercises. I realize now he probably felt left out. Tina and I always had each other, and he was odd man out, being the only boy and four years younger.

Of course, I am grateful for the wonders we saw: the Great Wall, the hidden warriors in Xian, the Emperor's palaces, Tiananmen Square, the Forbidden City, the beauty of Nanjing. When we finally reached Hong Kong, I thought my parents had died and gone to heaven. They sent the three of us out to dinner, and they dined in the hotel restaurant on salad, steaks, and a hearty Chardonnay. To this day, I have so many memories and stories about China, but mostly I am proud of Tina. As a twenty-two-year-old, she took on the enormous task of guiding us through a complicated and trying journey. She had to help navigate the language and our needs, complaints, and expectations.

## CHAPTER 10

# Hawaii and Beyond

Growing up, we were fortunate to take several trips to Hawaii. My parents fell in love with a resort called Kona Village, on the big island of Hawaii. We went for spring breaks and one time for Christmas. The resort was very old-style Polynesian; the property was dotted with large, upscale huts that were the rooms. Tina, Spencer, and I spent a lot of time together on these trips. My parents liked to drink mai tais under beach umbrellas and read books. Alexa would spend the day in the kids' camp, making Hawaiian crafts, and playing with kids her own age. There was a bar near the pool called the Shipwreck Bar; it was an old sailing ship turned into a bar. One afternoon, Tina and I were sipping virgin daiquiris at Shipwreck when a very handsome man turned toward Tina and in a low, sexy voice said, "Hi pretty lady. May I buy you a drink?" Tina blushed and said, "Thank you. That's so nice, but I am seventeen." The man was Lou Rawls. Lou Rawls was a famous R&B, gospel and soul singer, record producer, songwriter, and actor. He is probably best known for the song "You'll Never Find Another Love Like Mine." He thought Tina was gorgeous.

Our parents took just Tina and me for one spring break (freshman and sophomore years in college) to a different hotel on the Big Island. Tina was still at Dartmouth at the time. We shared a room. There was a very nice young man from Texas who showed an interest in Tina. She was not interested, and I knew it. Every afternoon we'd go back to our room and order the vegetable platter from room service. One afternoon, the phone rang, and it was him, asking for her. She was giving me the absolute stink eye when I said, "She's right here, and she would LOVE to speak to you."

She didn't want to be rude so she agreed to go to dinner with him. She was very mad at me. I was being a stinky little sister, and I knew it.

One day on that same trip, Tina and I were sitting down on the beach when I looked up from my book and saw four boys from Stanford walking toward us. I recognized one of them and turned beet red. Tina said, "Ing, you have to say hello." She pushed me toward them. So I did what she asked and, as it turned out, they were very friendly. The guy I knew was named Paul, and he was hosting the boys. His family owned a macadamia nut plantation in Waimea, a lush, mountainous region of Hawaii about thirty minutes away. He invited Tina and me to dinner. I'll never forget that night. Paul drove us in his jeep from the resort to his parents' home. As we drove up the mountain, Paul was blaring the album *The Look of Love* by the band ABC as we sang along to "The Look of Love" and "Be Near Me." We sat at a large table in an old Hawaiian home. His mom was an exotic Italian matriarch. Both his parents were so kind to Tina and me. It was one of the best experiences Tina and I had together during the college years. I wonder if spending time with those boys was another reason she chose to transfer to Stanford. It was an evening full of great company, conversation, and innocent flirting. The trade winds and floral fragrances of Hawaii are intoxicating, and that added to the allure of the evening.

When we returned to Stanford, we both happily spent time with those guys. It wasn't a competition, and because we were all friends, it worked. We would visit them in their fraternity house. I secretly had a crush on Paul, but so did about twenty other girls I knew. A few years after that, our whole family took another trip to the same resort. Tina and I had wonderful memories of that time she and I were there together and of our trip up to Waimea.

✳ ✳ ✳

After Tina graduated from Stanford, she followed my father's advice and went to work for Lindblad Travel, a pioneer in adventure travel. The trips attracted a high-end, educated clientele, and Tina helped lead tours on mainland China. At first, she was the junior guide; there was always an employee who had senior status on the trips. Her stories from these trips were so funny. There was a wealthy woman from New York City who had a pair of white jeans that shrunk in a hotel laundry load. She insisted that Tina find her the same pair, in a very remote part of China. Not possible. On one of these trips, the senior leader was a young man named Bill Messing. Bill was three years older and also attended Dartmouth, but they never knew each other there. They discovered as they talked that he had had an 8:00 am class and she had had a 9:00 am class in the same building. Bill said they must have passed each other three mornings a week going up and down the stairs, for an entire year. They fell in love and eventually moved to San Francisco together. I was thrilled, as I was living there post-college.

Spencer and Myra Clark

Ellen, Bob, Frank, Ruth Helsell

Bob, Linda at
engagement party

Ingrid and Tina at 1 and 2

Matching outfits

Spencer in elementary school

Helsell and Hoedemaker kids

Ingrid, Spencer and Tina

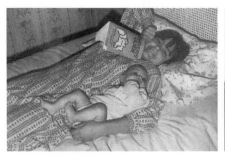
Ingrid with baby Alexa

Christmas morning

Tina and Alexa, Christmas

Ingrid and Tina,
Christmas

Happy Tina

Sad Tina

Jessica, Ingrid and Tina at Lakeside graduation

Stanford

Stanford graduation

Tina in China                    Ingrid, Tina at The Great
                                 Wall in China

Helsells in Hawaii          Hawaii: Eric, Alexa, Tina, Bill,
                                    Dad, Ingrid

Helsells 1984

Mink Island, Desolation Sound BC

Bohemia at the end of our dock

# Part 2: Tina (1986–2014)

CHAPTER 11

# San Francisco

Those were really, really happy years, when Tina and I were between the ages of twenty-two and twenty-six. For four years, we both lived in San Francisco and near enough to visit each other often. San Francisco, along with its many attractions, was our playground, and Tina and Bill included me often. One weekend, Bill asked us if we wanted to participate in an orienteering competition. He loved orienteering meets. The three of us piled into Tina's brown Jetta. It was a gorgeous day, and we drove across the Golden Gate Bridge to a course in the woods near Marin. Bill had registered himself for the advanced course and Tina and I for the beginner's course. Tina and I were handed our master map, compasses, and a brief explanation of how to find the controls. It's a treasure hunt in the woods. You are given a coordinate to find, along with a map and a compass. Off we went. We were excited, and we found the first control easily. The controls are usually orange and white marking flags, attached to a tree, a rock, a fallen limb. Feeling confident, we went in search of control number two. Found that one too. We thought we were very clever. We found numbers three, four, and five. It's a competition. You are supposed to do it as quickly as you can. We weren't racing, but we weren't dawdling. About to tackle the last control, we stopped for some water and a granola bar. Tina said, "C'mon Ing. Let's finish this." Off we went to find the sixth and final control. We ended up at a giant tree, but sadly, there was no control to be found. After about the fourth attempt, tromping through the woods, ending up near a marsh, we still found ourselves at that stupid tree. We got frustrated, started fighting.

Tina: "You don't know how to use the compass."

Ingrid: "No, you don't know how to use the compass."

Tina: "You have the map facing the wrong way."

Ingrid: "Now you are really starting to bug me!"

Suddenly, we just started laughing hysterically at ourselves, two Stanford graduates unable to use a map and compass correctly. Bill figured out we were lost and came to rescue us at that dumb tree. We made him help us find that sixth control. That was a really special day, being with Tina and Bill. It was full of adventure and friendship. On the drive back to San Francisco, I fell asleep, drifting off to the voices of two people I loved.

Tina and Bill also became fans of rollerblading. They would spend a couple of hours on weekend afternoons, rollerblading through Golden Gate Park. On one of these outings, I rented a pair and joined them. I found myself with Bill at the top of a rather large hill. Tina had already effortlessly raced down the hill, her long dark hair flowing behind her. I said, "Bill, I really don't know to stop in these skates." He showed me and said, "Ing, it's easy. Give it a try." I proceeded to take off, lost control, and wiped out in a nearby bush. I had some bloody scrapes all the way up one arm and leg. I never joined them again for rollerblading.

Bill and Tina lived near me in the Sunset District until the famous 6.9 Loma Prieta earthquake in 1989. That was an unforgettable day. I was sitting on the bus, going from work to home. At one point, a fellow passenger said. "Oh my God, there must have been a huge earthquake!" We were passing a small shopping center, and you could see glass breaking and people running into the streets. We didn't feel the earthquake because the bus was so heavy. When I got to my apartment, I was the only one home. A lamp had fallen over and two potatoes had rolled off the kitchen counter, but other than that, nothing else seemed amiss. Immediately, I worried about Tina. She was working in a high rise in the downtown area. Within about an hour, Bill showed up at my apartment. He hadn't heard from Tina either. The city was in chaos. Car alarms were blaring from the vibrations in the ground, and smoke could be seen from the fires in the Marina district. Smaller aftershocks happened all afternoon and into the night. It was beyond eerie. Finally, Tina arrived at my apartment. I cried when I saw her. Because the elevators shut down, she had to walk down many flights of stairs with her friend Jodi and another coworker who had a broken foot. They had to take it very slowly as they guided their injured friend down to the first floor. Within several days, their apartment (six blocks from mine) was deemed unsafe, and they had to move out within hours. I shared an apartment with two other women, and my room was connected to a tiny little room to the left, barely big enough for Tina and Bill's futon. They lived with us for a month. I loved having them with me.

The period following the earthquake was scary for so many people. I worked as a corporate concierge in the Bank of America building. My employer was the Shorenstein Company, one of the city's biggest developers. One of my clients from the Bank of America was killed in the overpass that collapsed in Oakland. He was such a nice man, and I grieved for his family, although I never met them.

During this same period, I went through a very painful breakup with a young man I had dated for six years. Tina was my savior. John was in my freshman dorm, but we didn't really meet until spring quarter. In hindsight, we should have broken up after six months. He was one of those people who gets under your skin. He grew up in Brigham City, Utah, raised by a Mormon mother and a non-Mormon father. He was not a good Mormon, and he didn't hide it. He was gorgeous (six foot four with bright blue eyes), highly intelligent, and very funny. As time went on, he became erratic with his interest in me. I've actually never met anyone like him since. He would become fascinated by something for an intense period of time, whether it was a person, a concept, a song even. I was it for about six months. He used to leave love poems on my schoolwork at Stanford's Green library. I'd return from the bathroom to find a poem. He wasn't in sight. It was a game we played, and it was romantic. He would follow me around. As the relationship progressed, he cheated on me numerous times.

The fall of my junior year, I went to Florence to study. Stanford had an amazing overseas program. John and I agreed to enjoy our time away, but there was no discussion about dating anyone else. In the 80s, there was no email or face-time. Mail took a long time to get from Palo Alto, California, to Florence, Italy. I received letters from John the first six weeks I was there, but then there was silence. For Thanksgiving, my friend Chris and I took an overnight train to Paris to meet Pierre and my friend Simone. Pierre was abroad in Germany, and Simone was studying in England. Pierre's family owned an apartment on the Left Bank where we stayed. Pierre and I found a time to call home. We both wanted to talk to Tina. After Tina and Pierre talked, I got on the line.

"Hi, Tina, I miss you!"

"I miss you too, Ing."

I asked, "Tina, I haven't heard from John in a long time. Do you ever see him on campus?" There was a long, uncomfortable pause.

"Oh, Ing. I asked John to call you several times. He has been dating a freshman girl."

"What? Who?" I asked.

"She's from Brazil, and she is a model."

I felt gutted. After we hung up, I cried and cried. I was a miserable companion in Paris to Chris, Pierre, and Simone.

After the long weekend, Chris and I took the train back to Florence. A day later, there was a call for me. It was John. He was very apologetic, but the hurt had been inflicted. After college, he and I lived together with some other Stanford friends on the island of Kauai, Hawaii. Later I discovered that the whole time we had been living there, he was writing to Emily, one of Tina's best friends, whom he had a crush on in college. He even invited her to come visit. Tina told me that. Although Tina and John were on friendly terms, Tina was wary of John's wanderings, while I kept believing he would change.

We broke up and reunited several times until my self-esteem tanked so badly that I had to end it. It took me a year of therapy and eventually a move back home to Seattle to heal. Once a week I would walk to my therapist's home. Her name was Jackie, and her office was in the basement and close to my apartment in San Francisco. After about a year, I told her I had the tools to move on. She said, "Ingrid, I think maybe we should talk about your mother." My response was, "That will require another entire year." She knew that the relationship with my mother was one of the reasons I clung to John so much, even when I knew the relationship had soured. When you grow up with emotional abuse, you tend to look for it again. I didn't think there was emotional abuse, but Jackie said his cheating and his periods of ignoring me were abusive. I don't blame John anymore. I blame myself for not reading the obvious signals that he had lost interest and lacking the confidence to walk away sooner. I really loved him.

Tina helped me so much through that period; I couldn't have done it without her. One day shortly after we broke up, he stopped by my apartment when Tina was with me. She met him at the door.

John said, "Hi, Tina. Can I come in and see Ingrid?"

"No. She is really hurting and can't see you for a while."

I was at the top of the stairs watching them. John knew that if Tina was with me and had the final word, he couldn't argue. Simply put, Bill and Tina were just always there for me. To this day, I love them both for that. Throughout the next couple of months, Tina and Bill would take me out to dinner, take me to the movies, and include me with their other friends. She was my older sister, my friend, my lioness, and I miss her being my protector. When sisters grow up with an unstable mother, they have to rely on each other.

# CHAPTER 12

# Tina and Bill

After Tina's break up with Pierre, she was tender for a few years. Bill came along at a time when she needed a companion. I'm a firm believer in the middle guy or middle girl. We all need someone who is safe for us after a painful breakup. Then we become brave again and seek someone who excites us, who challenges us. I had a middle guy between my six-year relationship and my husband Eric. I knew I would never marry my middle guy. Tina was crazy about Bill at the beginning, but then I began to see the cracks. She started to complain about aspects of his personality, that he wasn't funny, that he was always late. Instead of Bill Messing, she started to call him "Bill Missing."

Bill, the youngest of six children, was raised in Boston in a Catholic family. He went to Noble and Greenough High School in Massachusetts and then Dartmouth for college. He loved the outdoors and enjoyed hiking, skiing, kayaking, orienteering, and running. Although they both spoke Mandarin and loved China and their girls Sophie and Sylvie, in many ways, Tina and Bill were polar opposites. Whereas Bill loved to be active, Tina exercised sporadically, or if she really liked something. Tina was tidy; Bill was messy. Tina was very punctual. Bill was always late. Bill was a very happy person. For too much of her life, Tina wasn't happy.

Shortly after they had moved into an apartment together in San Francisco, Tina called me one late morning and said, "Ing, Bill was going to get some milk for our coffee at the corner store. He's been gone for three hours. Should I call the police?" I just laughed. I think he had discovered a street fair and was delighting in its goods.

Unlike Tina, Bill is a risk-taker. He was willing to risk losing money for investments, which may or may not have been successful. Tina was more financially cautious, and Bill's risk-taking made her very nervous.

Bill doesn't have an edge. Both Tina and I needed men with an edge. At Stanford, we were attracted to John and Pierre for a reason. When I say edge, I mean funny and a little irreverent. Turns out, their edges were too sharp, but we both loved and needed humor. As I've said, Bill had many talents, but he wasn't funny. Tina was funny.

After a few years living together, Bill asked Tina to marry him. About a month after their engagement, I asked her out to lunch. I said, "Tina, you are my sister and my closest friend. This is hard for me to say. Bill is an amazing guy. I know you love him, but I don't think you should marry him. You are really different people." She was quiet and then said, "Ingrid. You are such a bitch. How dare you tell me I shouldn't marry Bill. I love him." Lunch ended abruptly and then we didn't speak for weeks. Years later, when their marriage started to unravel, she said, "Ingrid, I remember that lunch. I should have listened to you."

They went ahead with their plans and were engaged in San Francisco but married at our parents' home in north Seattle in the summer of 1990. At this point, Tina and I had both left San Francisco. In the fall of 1990 I started a graduate program at Seattle University to get my masters in teaching. My parents sold our childhood home and moved to the Highlands when I was twenty-three. The Highlands represents wealth and status, and that's where my mom wanted to live. They set up a huge tent in the front yard, which had a sweeping view of Puget Sound and the Olympic mountains. The afternoon of the wedding, I was madly tying flowers to the tent poles. Tina came out in her bathrobe and curlers and barked a command at me, asking me to take care of another detail. I said, "Tina, I have to tie the flowers on the poles first." She was a happy but bossy bride. I was also crabby because I had gained a good ten pounds and could not fit into my maid of honor dress. When I tried it on and couldn't zip it, Tina laughed so hard. "It's not funny, Tina. I'm fat! I can't zip up the dress!" Luckily, two days before the wedding, I was able to go to the boutique and exchange the dress for a bigger size. Tina and I used to chuckle about that. We were both at our heaviest at each other's weddings. My wedding was in July 1993, just two months after Tina and Bill had their first child, Sophie. On that beautiful, warm August evening, Tina and Bill began their life together as husband and wife. It was a fabulous party with an awesome band.

My first indication that Tina's depression was worse than I ever knew was after they returned from their honeymoon. They went to Antigua in the Caribbean. I phoned her. "How was the honeymoon?!" Her response, "Well, I spent hours every day crying in a hammock on the beach." She cried on her honeymoon because she knew Pierre and Hilary were about to be married.

Years after Pierre and Tina had broken up, Pierre and Hilary started dating. They were both living in Boston. They got engaged, and their wedding date was the week after Tina and Bill's. Tina became obsessive about their relationship. She was hurt, mad, and unyielding. I could not understand why she couldn't let it go. They hadn't dated in years, and Pierre and Hilary always had a spark for each other. Whenever she and I got together after the honeymoon, she could only talk about Pierre and Hilary's relationship. She would say, "I just don't understand why they have to marry each other. It's so cruel. They were both my good friends. I bet he always liked her more than he liked me." Tina's obsession with their marriage was unrelenting and exhausting. Not until later did I discover that her emotional reactions—that her good friends had abandoned her— were indicative of borderline personality disorder.

The irony is that years later, Bill, Tina, Hilary, and Pierre spent several great vacations together with their children. Tina was able to move past the hurt and eventually they all enjoyed each other. Over the years, Tina kept in close touch with Hilary and Pierre. They flew in from Boston to attend her memorial. It was so comforting to see them after such a long time. Seven years after her death, they still check in on me on my birthday, Tina's birthday, and on New Year's Eve. Tina would have delighted in the fact that they recently became grandparents of twin boys. Tina loved their four children; their youngest two are fraternal twins. It's yet another beautiful life event that Tina has not witnessed. Pierre has kept all the letters Tina wrote him when they were dating.

## CHAPTER 13

# Pacific Rim Resources

After her stint with Lindblad Travel, Tina went to work as a strategy consultant for a small, boutique consulting firm in San Francisco called Pacific Rim Resources. Recalling Tina's performance, president and CEO of PRR (1988–2002), Julie, said, "Tina was an incredible member of my team. She was excellent at translating me and my visions to everyone else. She was incredibly gifted at breaking things down and taking disparate information and pulling all the components together. She was an articulate and gifted writer." An example of a project was one that involved assessing the Chinese market for ball bearings. In order to gather all the information for that project, Tina had to generate bottoms-up research spanning numerous industries. Tina would travel to China and usually be gone about two weeks. While there, her research required a complete analysis of organizational structure, government entities' involvement, county and/or national level involvement, and any regulatory bodies. She would gather all this information and bring it back to San Francisco to write a highly detailed report for the client on ball bearing production in China. Julie added that travel in China was difficult at this time. There were no cell phones or zoom meetings. Flights were limited. If you had to travel to China for business, it was a lengthy stay.

When I asked Julie about Tina's ability to converse in Mandarin, she said, "Tina's linguistic capabilities weren't even her strongest suit. She was a thinker and excellent at managing people. In the consulting world, the eventual goal is to manage your own clients." Julie added, "Tina preferred to stand behind the lines. She didn't want to have her own clients. Instead, she began to train and develop the junior staff at Pacific Rim Resources in exactly how to be an excellent consultant."

Tina worked at PRR from 1990 to 1998 in San Francisco and from Seattle until just after she and Bill had Sylvie. Frequently, Julie asked Tina to do contract work. One of these jobs was a project for the Stanford Business School. Julie was asked to develop a strategy and figure out how Stanford Business School could have a presence in China. Tina and another Chinese consultant were Julie's favorite people to hire. Julie knew every project Tina touched would be exceptional. Julie also said that Tina never showed signs of depression. She only ever saw the productive, brilliant Tina.

CHAPTER 14

# Raising Children

The happiest time in our adult lives together as sisters was when our children were young. We shared so much together during those years. We loved each other's children so much. We also continued to bond over the mental health of our mom and how exhausting her behaviors were. In my first year of marriage, Mom went through an intense manic phase. She invited some of her close friends to a luncheon at her home. She wanted to convince them to invest in a card-making company. On a trip to Hawaii, Mom apparently had met someone who worked for Madonna. She showed him her gift cards, and he told her he thought Madonna might really be interested. I'm not confident that interaction ever happened in Hawaii. Tina was at the luncheon, and I was not. I had a commitment, and I didn't really want to see my mom humiliate herself. And she did: Tina said the luncheon was embarrassing. So, we bonded over being mothers and having a mother whose illness was hard to live with, even in our mid-thirties. We also continued our fun phone conversations. When Tina was on a roll describing something or somebody she found amusing, she was the best. It always added some chuckles and sparkles to my day.

If you told me when Tina was in her thirties that she would die by suicide at 51, I would never have believed you. Throughout the years, she sought and received therapy for her depression. With therapy and medicine for depression and anxiety, she lived a very full life. She and Bill welcomed Sophie on May 26, 1993, and then Sylvie on December 23, 1998. We had two sons by then, Henry and George, and then our last child, Hazel, was born June 23, 2001. When Sophie was born, she and Bill were renting a home in the Madrona neighborhood. I was a fourth-grade teacher at Madrona Elementary. Almost every day after school, I would go visit Tina and Sophie. I would hold Sophie while Tina worked or did chores. I was in awe of beautiful, dark-eyed Sophie and couldn't believe Tina was a mom.

Tina and I both suffered from post-partum depression after our children were born. My mom had suffered from post-partum depression with Alexa, so perhaps it was genetic. Our Henry had his days and nights mixed up. He would take two three-hour naps during the day and be up every two hours, wanting to eat at night. I had a difficult birth with him, with hours and hours of labor. He wouldn't budge, so then I had a C-section. At the hospital, a social worker met with a group of new moms. They covered post-partem issues and said if you ever had thoughts of hurting your child, it was time to get help. After about a month of being up most of the night, I held him and pondered, "If I strangled him, would Eric know?" Immediately, I burst into tears, woke up Eric, asked him to take Henry. I got the help I needed, my depression cleared, and I was able to love him fully. Tina had a very similar situation with Sophie, and we bonded over how hard it had been. Fortunately, neither of us had postpartum depression with Sylvie, George, or Hazel. I will forever be grateful to Brooke Shields for bringing her post-partum experience to the world. It was a courageous move for a public figure. The declaration of her struggles was a gift to new mothers everywhere.

Tina was delighted by our boys. Henry and George called her "Teeta," Henry's name for her when he was little. As they grew up, they could make her laugh harder than anyone. Their boy antics—sword play, loud farting, and crude jokes—were hilarious to her. Like Tina, Henry is an amazing mimic and can do any voice, so they entertained each other all the time. It was fun that she had two girls and I had two boys. Then we were given the gift of Hazel, so we could experience raising a girl as well. We took fun family trips together to our parents' beach cabin on Whidbey Island. Page and her two sons, Hale and Robert, would join us too, as her family had a home nearby. Tina and I talked on the phone at least once a day, sometimes up to four times per day. She would often answer the phone with a funny voice, or pick up and say, "Yello." We talked about diapers, sleep deprivation, then the terrible twos, the start of preschool, then kindergarten, etc. There was always so much to share. We gathered for many, many family holidays.

One February winter break, Tina and I decided to go to Victoria, British Columbia, for a few nights, kids in tow. We took the Clipper ship from Seattle, which is a very fast ferry boat. Our kids were between the ages of five and twelve, Sophie the oldest, Hazel the youngest. It wasn't the dream getaway we had hoped for. The weather was dreary, the kids were tough. One afternoon, we had high tea at the Empress which is a famous hotel in the heart of the city. After a few minutes of being seated, Sylvie looked at her tea and gave out a little shriek. She said, "There is something in my tea!" The tea was coagulating, all lumpy. Sophie and Henry started laughing. They had bought some potion at a magic store and put it in Sylvie's teacup. At first, Tina and I both giggled a bit, but I soon realized how upset Sylvie was, and I reprimanded Henry.

That trip highlighted a few things for me. Tina had brought a babysitter along, to help out. She paid for a separate hotel room for the sitter. I thought it was strange, as the two of us could have handled the kids. Also, after the tea incident, we both scolded Sophie and Henry. Directly afterward, Tina went shopping with Sophie and bought her a bunch of clothes. Tina loved her girls so much but tough parenting was hard for her. She started to pay for a lot of help, and it reminded me of my mom. She and Bill also didn't like to discipline much. Hence the shopping reward after the tea incident? That was their choice, but it started making outings with our families hard. Eric and I did have consequences for bad behavior.

As our children grew up, my relationship with Tina grew more complicated. We started this pattern that was very destructive. If we had an argument about something, we would start a nasty email chain, flinging unkind words at each other. We had traded words for wooden clogs. But then, Tina would stonewall me. She would stop talking to me for weeks at a time, sometimes months. Something I said or did would set her off and, instead of talking to me about it, she would shut down. I take half of the blame for this pattern, but it hurt me so much, and it didn't seem to affect her. I always came crawling back, apologized first. When Tina's girls were six and two, she and Bill had planned a trip to Italy for the spring of 2000. A group of Dartmouth friends were going together. In the fall of 1999, she asked me if I could take the girls but said she would send along their nanny as well. I said, "Yes, we can take the girls, but I don't need your nanny." It was set that Eric and I would have Sophie and Sylvie for ten days that spring. With or without the nanny hadn't been decided.

As the year 2000 approached and people were making plans for the millennium, Eric and I were invited to a party in Sun Valley, Idaho, with a large group of Eric's friends from college. I had arranged childcare for Henry and George for December 29 and 30 but couldn't find anyone for New Year's Eve. I emailed Tina, knowing she and Bill didn't have big plans. "Hey Tina, is there any chance you could take Henry and George for New Year's? I have coverage for the first two nights." Her response was, "Oh, so it's OK that you get invited to a big party in Sun Valley, but Bill and I have to stay home and watch our kids and yours on the millennium?!" I was dumbfounded. We had recently agreed to a long stay for her kids at our home. Tina felt insulted that I even asked. We didn't speak for at least a month after that. She also found someone else to watch their girls while they were in Italy.

This pattern continued for years, and looking back, it followed the escalation of her illness. Again, her angry response was indicative of borderline personality disorder. People with BPD feel things in extremes and often can't see any middle ground. The sicker she became, the worse the stonewalling was. Eventually, we agreed not to have conversations over email. I urged her to pick up the phone and talk to me. We would be good for a while, but the pattern always kicked in. During these times, I was not a saint either. I can be hotheaded and unforgiving at times. The difference between her and me was that it really upset me when we weren't talking. I always felt a little lost when I couldn't speak to her. She was my touchstone. She was capable of tuning me out with seemingly little concern. Also, she was averse to apologizing. It was like an allergy for her. Tina was never officially diagnosed with borderline personality disorder, but since her death, I have done quite a bit of research, and there is so much of the diagnosis that makes sense with her behavior patterns.

# CHAPTER 15

# Borderline Personality Disorder/Depression

The main characteristic of BPD is the difficulty in being able to regulate emotions. People with BPD tend to feel emotions intensely and for long periods of time. According to NAMI, the National Alliance on Mental Illness, patients have "impulsivity, poor self-image, and stormy relationships." Below is a list of symptoms:

- Frantic efforts to avoid real or imagined abandonment by friends and family.

- Unstable personal relationships that alternate between idealization ("I'm so in love!") and devaluation ("I hate her"). This is also sometimes known as "splitting."

- Distorted and unstable self-image, which affects moods, values, opinions, goals, and relationships.

- Impulsive behaviors that can have dangerous outcomes, such as excessive spending, unsafe sex, reckless driving, or misuse or overuse of substances.

- Self-harming behavior including suicidal threats or attempts.

- Periods of intense depressed mood, irritability, **or anxiety lasting a few hours to a few days.**

- Chronic feelings of boredom or emptiness.

- Inappropriate, intense, or uncontrollable anger—often followed by shame and guilt.

- Dissociative feelings—disconnecting from your thoughts or sense of identity or "out of body" type of feelings—and stress-related paranoid thoughts. Severe cases of stress can also lead to brief psychotic episodes.

At different points in her life, Tina displayed all of these symptoms. Recall Tina in the hammock at thirteen, the intense sadness post honeymoon, the anger at Pierre and Hilary, the email wars with me. What really, really saddens me is that after all the therapy she had, how did the experts miss it?

Whenever I've been to a therapist, they always probe and probe about my mom being bipolar. I understand doctors have to rule it out. Neither I nor Tina was found to suffer from bipolar disorder though we both experienced depression and anxiety. As Tina always said to me, "Ing, I never experience the high highs. I only experience the low lows."

After Tina died, Catherine Monk took my father and me to lunch. She said, "I feel like my profession failed Tina." I agree. After Tina died, I came across a YouTube video about severe depression given by a Stanford professor named Robert Saponsky. The lecture aired on November 10, 2009. Saponsky begins the lecture by saying that depression is "crippling" and "pervasive" in the US and that by 2025, it will be the number two cause of disability in our country. He goes on to describe different levels of depression and puts the illness into three basic categories:

1. Everyday feelings of sadness that come and go and are not debilitating. We all experience these feelings.

2. The kind of depression that is a reaction to a major event like the loss of a job, a hard move, or the death of a loved one. I definitely experienced this after Tina died.

3. Major depression, which is a biological condition like diabetes or heart disease. In Saponsky's words, "It's a biochemical disorder with a genetic component in early experience influences where someone cannot appreciate sunsets."

Saponsky emphasizes that severe depression is a biological disorder.

Tina also definitely experienced a condition Saponsky refers to as psychomotor retardation, which is a characteristic of being severely depressed. This is when every task is utterly exhausting. In the years leading up to her death, I would encourage her just to take a walk with me, for ten minutes, but she would always say, "Ingrid, you just don't understand. It is too exhausting to even take a shower." Her depression followed what Saponsky describes as "rhythmic patterns," when she could get very, very low for a month or two, come out of it, and then perhaps a year later, she would experience the same pattern. She had a debilitating illness. Tina used to say, "Ing, I would rather have cancer than depression because a lot of cancers can be cured." What continues to amaze me is that despite those patterns and extreme physical discomfort, for such a great deal of her life, she was productive, creative, loving, funny, and caring.

Part of her illness was that she never thought she was good enough, smart enough, thin enough. She also didn't believe anybody liked her, which was very untrue. She was adored by many people. Tina received a lot of attention for her beauty. As the years crept on, she really struggled with aging. As her friend Catherine writes,

> She was so beautiful and her appearance garnered all sorts of attention, attention that is hard to always match. And beauty does fade with age. To not get the same attention as a mature woman as she did routinely as a young one, that is hard; it is hard to lose that adoration to which one literally, easily gets addicted. I think this was a stunning blow to Tina, a constant message from the world that she didn't measure up, and that hurt.

Everyone's beauty fades with time. But for Tina, aging did take a toll. She talked about it a lot. She loved to quote Deborah Harry's song "Die young . . . stay pretty."

She constantly struggled with her weight too. Often, she would ask me, "Ingrid, am I as big as that woman over there?" I hated that question because if she was, I lied and said, "Of course, you aren't." She always used to say, "I never lost a pound that I didn't meet again." I have adopted that line for myself. One day, we were doing errands and we stopped to fill up her car. I noticed she looked different, brighter. "Tina, did you get Botox?" "Yes! Isn't it great?" We were in our early forties, and I thought it was a little young to start. That was the beginning of her quest to constantly improve her looks.

As Tina aged, I started to recognize such similar patterns between her and my mom. They were both severely depressed. But being bipolar, our mom did have the high highs that Tina never experienced. Mom and Tina must have always felt like they were swimming upstream.

# CHAPTER 16

# Tina's Talents

Tina was a remarkably talented human being and a very hard worker. When she still worked at Pacific Rim Resources, her long journeys to and from mainland China were hard on her and her family. She would be away for several weeks and then return and have to adjust to a new time zone. On one of her business trips, Sophie became quite ill. She was just two, and as Bill says, "She had a misguided immune system." She had to be admitted to Seattle Children's Hospital. I remember being at the hospital with Bill and Sophie, and Tina would phone in when the time zones allowed. She was so worried about Sophie, and helpless to do anything from ten thousand miles away. At one point, Sophie was getting worse, and Bill told Tina she should come home. Tina left China, flew home, and went directly to the hospital. Fortunately, steroid treatment worked and Sophie fully recovered.

Whether it was a new skill, volunteer work, a piece of writing, or making jewelry, Tina attacked each with precision and gusto. As with every artistic endeavor she tried, her jewelry was beautiful. She bought a silver clay kiln and started making her own earrings and pendants. She worked with silver and taught herself bead and wirework. She created a website, and she had several small shows. I hosted one at my home and invited a lot of my friends, and they still wear the necklaces they bought. Her pieces were unlike any jewelry I've seen. For example, she would build a silver chain for a necklace, and then she would accentuate it with a showstopper like an unusual, colorful stone, or an antique pendant. She searched high and low for these treasures, in Seattle craft stores, antique stores, online. Every time I wear one of her necklaces or earrings, I have women ask me about them.

She also dressed beautifully. She was a fan of black pants, soft, expensive cashmere sweaters, and flat shoes. She accentuated her outfits with exquisite scarves and unusual jewelry. She had a love for expensive handbags. She definitely channeled Gaga and Mom in her love of fashion. She always found the perfect gifts for her family and friends. She knew I loved the color pink. One year for Christmas, she gave me a pink Burberry scarf. I wear it all the time. Back then, it would have been a luxury for me to buy that. Before wrapping gifts in cloth became popular (and better for the environment), Tina wrapped her gifts in cloth or would buy a scarf as part of the gift and wrap the rest in the scarf. I always looked forward to her gifts! She had a keen eye for decorating, from her first apartment in San Francisco to the home she was renting when she died. Because of her travel to China and her ability to speak Mandarin, her homes always had an Asian flair. One time after having dinner at Tina's house, Eric and I were driving home. He said, "Ing, don't take this badly, but you did not inherit your sister's ability to decorate." He was right. She could have easily been a successful interior designer.

Tina wrote beautifully, with cadence, style, and humor. She loved to write, whether it was a report for work, a personal letter, a funny email. Her voice was strong. She often interjected humor when appropriate. I asked her once to help me update my resume. This requires a little background. We raised our children on an 88-acre piece of property where Eric grew up. Eventually, Eric and all three of his siblings ended up living on the property. His parents lived in the middle. My father-in law, Pete, and Eric's sister, Molly, were horse lovers. Hence, there were horses. I am allergic, afraid, and have never been a fan. Occasionally someone would leave a gate open, and a horse or two would escape. They would run all over our property, ripping up the lawn with their hooves. This was a nightmare for me, and I always had to call Pete or Molly to get the horses back in their pasture. Tina knew I hated this. As I was reading through my resume after Tina revised it, I read under "professional accomplishments": "I am an excellent wrangler and have a deep passion for horses."

Tina was very active with the Epiphany School, a small private school in their neighborhood that Sophie and Sylvie attended from pre-kindergarten to the sixth grade. What started as Tina chairing the safari-themed auction led to her being on the board and, eventually, becoming the board president. During her tenure, she was responsible for leading the search to find a new head of school. She also led a seven-million-dollar capital campaign to build an additional wing to the school. Alexa, Mark, and their children live in the Madrona neighborhood where Tina used to live and where Epiphany is. Every time I drive past Epiphany school, I am reminded of Tina, and I am proud of her.

She would also take on major projects and do them flawlessly. For years, our hospital guild hosted an annual family dinner dance in Seattle. We called it the Seattle Snow Ball. Tina took on the job of handling the guests' registrations, meal choices, and payments. She had organized, impressive systems for procedures.

Catharine, a woman in our hospital guild and a good friend of both Tina and mine, wrote our family an incredible letter after she died. Here is an excerpt:

> I thought Tina was among the most capable, impressive people I knew, and on so many occasions her perception, conviction, and humility took my breath away. I was the first-ever chair of the Seattle Snow Ball, a role far outside my comfort zone, and one in which I would have experienced no success without Tina's constantly dependable encouragement. Unsurprisingly, Tina leapt forward to chair the second Snow Ball. While I relished the chance to support her, that summer I was diagnosed with cancer and could not even attend. So she sent me a barrage of hilarious email updates, keeping me connected, smiling, and occasionally immobilized with laughter.

Tina asked Catharine to join the Epiphany School Board with her. Catharine says, "I loved that she saw potential in me, that she would be both mentor and ally." In her letter, she added, "Tina lived with an integrity, an honor, which humbles me. She gave until she had no more to give. For all the sacrifices, the many ways she contributed during her life, I as a friend feel the lasting difference she made. My time with her, while too short, was a reprieve, a favor, a blessing. I continue to listen to who she is, for all that she hopes."

So many of Tina's closest friends have helped me through this grief, mostly by talking about her and being vulnerable about their huge sense of loss. Several years after Tina died, our guild gathered. We started to talk about Tina. I looked over and saw some tears spilling down Catharine's cheeks, and she said, "I just can't talk about her."

Coinciding with Tina's talents and many feats, however, was the beginning of Tina's downward spiral. The years between 2006 and her death in 2014 are the hardest to write about. To understand one of her major triggers, it's important to write about the demise of their finances.

# CHAPTER 17

# The Financial Collapse

Bill's career has taken many twists and turns. Like Tina, he has a propensity for new projects and goals. After Dartmouth, he went to work for Lindblad, where he met Tina. After that, he worked as a managing editor for Harper Collins Publisher, specifically on the *Day in the Life* series. The books were coffee-table sized works of art, with huge photographs, and each book represented a twenty-four-hour period in that specific country. Photographers were sent to each country, and each had a particular region to capture. Bill started with "A Day in the life of China," and then did a "Day in the Life of Italy." He continued with books about Ireland and Hollywood. With Sophie on the way, Bill went looking for a job in Seattle, and he landed at Bill Gates' company Interactive Home Systems. It was sold to Microsoft, where for nearly ten years, Bill worked in consumer services, primarily interactive TV and MSN. He created the web portal at msn.com.

Between Tina's work at Pacific Rim Resources and Bill's at Microsoft, they did very well financially. They were able to buy a piece of property in Seattle's Madrona neighborhood and built a custom home. They took nice vacations, particularly to Scottsdale, Arizona, where they had a timeshare at the Four Seasons. Tina loved the desert beauty and solitude of Arizona. During those years, Tina was always so generous. Whenever we had a meal, she always picked up the check. Money became important to Tina. I think it gave her a sense of stability and having it made her feel powerful. In 2003, Bill left Microsoft to go work for the startup company Classmates. com, an internet platform for finding classmates from high school and college. He was the vice president of production and programming.

Despite Bill's success at all these companies, his dream was always to be an entrepreneur. In 2006, he started his own company. The concept was basically a platform similar to Facebook, but it had musical components. Tina and Bill put a lot of their own finances into the venture, and Bill was very successful in getting major investors, family amongst them. When the economic crash of 2008 hit right before the business was poised to go to market, everything fell apart. Tina's anxiety over the business not being successful was the catalyst that drove her into another pattern of deep depression that she never recovered from. In Bill's words, "Tina lost her sense of security, and she was never able to get it back." For the next six years, her zest for life faded. Her behavior became erratic.

I watched my sister slowly unravel. I was proud of Tina and Bill for taking such a risk, for Bill venturing out to be his own boss, which he had always wanted. But I wasn't part of the marriage and didn't realize how much they had suffered financially. Tina had recently taken a position as the director of development for the Recovery Café in Seattle, a treatment center for homeless individuals who need help with addiction recovery and the opportunity to rebuild their lives. The Recovery Café was started in 2003 by Killian Noe, a compassionate, intelligent, and visionary woman, who saw the desperate need for people who struggle with mental health and addiction and don't have a home of their own. Tina had the utmost respect for Killian, and Tina liked her position there, but her salary was meant only to supplement their lives, not be the major source, so the family was in a financial pinch. Also, Tina was heading down her own road of addiction, so it probably wasn't the best place to work. At this point, I was encouraging Tina to use her Mandarin and jump back into the Asian market, but she adamantly refused. Repeatedly she said, "I do not know how to speak Mandarin anymore." If she had been mentally stable, I am quite certain that is exactly what she would have done. She refused to take the steps to improve their situation. So, it wasn't just depression. It was also stubbornness.

Their financial slide was very hard on my relationship with Tina. Eric and I had decided that I would be a stay-at-home mother, and with three children close in age, my life was very busy. Eric and I have a traditional marriage in that way. He was responsible for our finances. I was responsible for the daily lives of our children. Tina became envious of our lifestyle and then our marriage. Our marriage hasn't been perfect, but Eric and I have a strong foundation and deep love for one another. I've talked to Page about this a lot. Page says that Tina always talked fondly about me and us, but that there was envy. My relationship with Tina was a mixture of love, protection, humor, but it was also fraught with envy, she of me and me of her, at different points and different times. Perhaps that's what happens when you are born seventeen months apart and your mom is too mired in her own sadness to celebrate each child's attributes. Another event that drove Tina deeper into depression was her decision to have an affair.

## CHAPTER 18

# The Affair

In the winter of 2012, Tina asked me to meet her for coffee. I was always eager to meet up when she wasn't stonewalling me. We met at the Hi-Spot Café in the Madrona neighborhood by her home. It had been my favorite breakfast/coffee spot for years since I landed my first teaching job at Madrona Elementary, one block away. Often, I would rush in and grab a latte and a blueberry muffin before I tackled the challenge of teaching twenty-eight fourth graders for the day. Over the years Tina, Alexa and I would meet there. When I walked in, Tina was seated near the coffee bar, at a table for two by the window. She got up, and we hugged. When I sat down, I knew by her expression that she was hurting and wanted to tell me something.

"Ing, I have something I need to tell you. I have been dreading telling you about it for months, but I just need to share it with you."

"OK," I said.

She cleared her throat, paused a moment, and then said, "I had an affair."

One of my best and worst qualities is that I show all expression on my face. I can show joy just as easily as I can show despair, fear, or disappointment. I am certain that my face expressed both despair and disappointment.

"I knew you would react like that."

"Tina, I am just shocked. I mean, I know you and Bill are unhappy. How did it happen? When?"

The details started to unfold. Alexa lived in New York City from 2003 to 2011. In the last two years, she was in graduate school for Landscape

Architecture at City College of New York. In May of 2010, Mom, Dad, Tina, Eric, and I went to her graduation. We all had different times and days when we departed. Mom and Dad left a day before Eric and I did. Tina stayed a few extra days to visit Page and her family in their home in Tuxedo Park, New York. When we landed in Seattle on Sunday evening, there was a voice mail from my dad: "Ing, it's Dad. Alexa had a panic attack. She is having a really hard time, just having graduated and dealing with the unknown of what lies ahead. If you and Eric are still in the city, can you please go to her apartment?" I called him back to say: "Hi Dad, it's Ing. We just landed in Seattle, but Tina is still in New York." So, Dad contacted Tina, and she said she would stay with Alexa for a few days after her stay in Tuxedo.

In Alexa's words: "Tina came back to my little apartment from Tuxedo a different person. She was uplifted and talking about this guy she met who was a friend of Page and Pete's. I didn't really know what to say, so I just listened, knowing that she had been so unhappy with Bill. I wanted to be supportive of her feeling somewhat different." Alexa's reaction would have been different from mine. She was twenty-nine and single at the time. Tina and I were forty-five and forty-six, both married, with five children between us.

Tina had met Dave at a dinner at Page's home in Tuxedo Park. He was a friend of her husband Pete's from high school. They grew up in Astoria, Oregon. As Page noted,

> An old childhood friend of Pete's from Oregon (to
> use the term "friend" loosely, he didn't even make the cut
> to attend our wedding.") happened to be in New York, and
> Pete invited him up to our house. He was in the military,
> specializing in intelligence gathering, interrogating suspects
> in Iraq. He bragged a great deal about his work, which told
> me he was full of shit. People I know who actually worked
> in interrogation would NEVER talk about it. Dave is a very
> fit guy and looks like someone who works out all the time.

He was an Army Ranger, so [he] had the buzz cut. He is not
a handsome guy by any means, just a generic, meaty guy,
but I could tell Tina was attracted to him. In her defense, he
immediately lasered in on her and gave her so much attention, both physical (sitting super close to her) and flirting.
She was vulnerable to his attention because she and Bill
were in a lull. By Monday, Dave offered her a ride to the
airport.

Despite the attraction between Tina and Dave, Page never dreamt
that they would have an affair. A year after meeting him, Tina called
Page and said, "I have something to tell you. Are you sitting down?" She
then proceeded to tell her about their affair. Page told me that Tina was
helping Dave with a lawsuit he was fighting. He would be appreciative of
Tina's help and then he would ghost her, and she'd be devastated. Then he
would reappear in her life. Tina told me they met for two or three covert
weekends. I am not certain of the cities, but I know they met in Boston
once, and I believe, Portland.

As I was digesting all of this, Tina added, "The worst part of the affair
happened after the first weekend we were together. When I was seated
on the airplane returning to Seattle, something distinctly snapped in my
brain. An immediate, intense depression washed over me, and I have been
intensely depressed ever since then."

I asked, "Do you think it was because you felt guilty?"

She responded, "Yes, that was a huge part of it." Then the conversation turned toward the fact that they had stopped seeing each other. "Can
you believe he dumped me? I know it's wrong, but I really liked him. I
am so sad."

"Tina, what do you mean he dumped you? You are acting like you
are a couple. You are married."

"I know, it's not rational. Now he's dating a blonde woman with really
big boobs. And she looks like she's really stupid."

"How do you know that?"

"I follow him on Facebook." She started crying. "Ingrid, what do you think she has that I don't?" It was the side of Tina that always broke my heart. She never felt good enough, loved enough, special enough.

"This is crazy talk, Tina. You are married. I know you guys are struggling, but I know that Bill still loves you and that you love Bill. Are you going to tell him about the affair?"

"No! I am never going to tell him. I have talked to Page about it, and she said, 'No! Work on your marriage and live with your guilt.' As Dear Abby says, 'confessing only serves the confessor.' Ingrid, it will only hurt him. Besides, it's over."

"Hmm. Well, I really don't appreciate that you told me because every time I see Bill, I will have this knowledge. I wish you hadn't told me. I think you owe it to Bill to tell him."

We sat in silence for a while. Things were worse between Tina and Bill than I knew. She never told him about the affair.

*** *** ***

About two weeks after Tina died, Bill had the unenviable task of going through her rental house, closing out her life. He found some torn-out pages from her journal that she had thrown into a wastebasket. On the pages were Tina's words about Dave, the affair, the end of the relationship, and the tremendous guilt she felt. After he read it, he called me. The conversation went something like this:

"Hi, Ingrid. So, as you know I am going through all of Tina's possessions, and I just found a journal entry about a guy Tina had an affair with? Ingrid, did you know about it?" I had always dreaded this moment, and I thought it would come someday.

"Yes, she told me about it after it had ended. I asked her to tell you, but she chose not to. She knew it would hurt you. I am so sorry you had to find out about it this way." Bill is not an angry person, but I could hear the pain in his voice. Afterward, he also called Page to ask her about the affair.

Not only did Bill have to clean up the physical part of Tina's life, but he had to deal with the tremendous emotional fallout, this secret included.

✶ ✶ ✶

To relieve her intense stress about money, the affair, and the tremendous guilt she felt, Tina turned to alcohol and increased her anti-anxiety meds. Until she was about 40, Tina never really drank. She and Bill would come to family events with a six-pack of dark beer, and they would usually share just one. In her early forties, Tina told me she had discovered Chardonnay and loved it. At family gatherings, she would drink too much and become belligerent. I started to fear having her to dinners because her behavior could get nasty. At one point, I asked Dad to have a conversation with Tina about her drinking and her behavior at family dinners, and he did talk to her. There would be periods where she didn't drink as much but, eventually, she would fall back into an ugly pattern, and the entire family was always wary about where the evening would go.

Before she went to rehab, Tina was taking 300 mg of Xanax a day, which is quite a lot considering that 25 mg is a more typical dosage. I don't know how she functioned at all. Xanax is a benzodiazepine, used to treat anxiety and panic disorders. I went through a very dark winter when I was forty-seven and was prescribed Xanax. I was amazed at how quickly my brain calmed down. I also knew that it tends to be addictive and therefore couldn't be a long-term substitute for my anxiety. I took it for about five months. I was taking 25 mg a day.

"Benzos" are over-prescribed in our country. Doctors hand them out like M&Ms. Meditation, yoga, mindfulness, breathing, exercise, and healthy food are all remedies for anxious minds. I commend all of those in the medical profession who discuss these non-habit-forming methods with their patients.

CHAPTER 19

# The Cayman Islands and ECT

One of the highlights of Tina's life was her annual trip to the Cayman Islands, south of Cuba and northwest of Jamaica. They consist of three islands, Grand Cayman being the largest. Those Cayman trips follow a parallel pattern of Tina before her illness, and after. Tina's friend Sally Schwartz from Dartmouth was the hostess. Her parents owned a three-bedroom condo at the Coral Stone Club, located on Seven Mile Beach next to the Ritz Carleton on Grand Cayman. I've seen photos. It is a glorious setting with white sand and a turquoise ocean. The year Tina turned forty, Sally invited college friends for a celebratory week. What began as a fortieth birthday trip turned into an annual event. It started as a get-together for college friends, but as the years went on, the group changed, and by the tenth year, Tina and Sally were the only Dartmouth girls. Tina looked forward to this spring trip every year. It was her chance to reconnect with close friends. Eventually, Sally even handed the planning over to Tina and another woman. They would email Sally's father's assistant and then coordinate the flights. The women walked the beach, ate fabulous dinners, swam, drank, and swapped stories about marriage, careers, and motherhood. Tina would always come back, kissed by the Caribbean sun, aglow and rejuvenated. At the apex of her life, Tina raved about the Caymans, but everything changed in 2011.

In April, 2011, Tina went, as usual, to Cayman. A few days into the trip, Tina sent me an email. She said, "It's awful here. Sally and her rich friends shop online all day for furniture for their second homes." As Sally explained to me, she had very wealthy friends whose husbands had worked as consultants, made fortunes, and retired early. Her parents owned the condo, but she did not have a second home. In fact, one of the things Sally and Tina shared at this point were confessions about their unhappy marriages, and the stress of living with men who were struggling financially in their respective startup companies. Tina was envious, as her own financial situation had changed drastically. The online shopping was a trigger.

Sally also recalls the 2011 trip as one when Tina spent a lot of time in her room during the day, reminiscent of their winter semester together in New York City. When Tina returned home, I called her the next morning. "How was the trip?" She said, "I am so depressed that in my layover at my Chicago hotel, I researched ways to kill myself." I think my heart stopped and bile formed in my mouth. I told Tina to put Bill on the phone immediately. She said, "He's in the shower." I said, "I don't care. Put him on, or else I'm driving there." We lived thirty minutes apart. Bill came on the line, and I told him what she had said. I insisted she needed help, and she needed it right away.

Of course, Bill knew about Tina's depression, but these extreme thoughts scared him too. He called 911. They took her to Swedish Hospital on Cherry Hill in Seattle, and from the ER, she was transferred to the psychiatric ward. This was the beginning of the fear I started to feel every single day. I myself was going through an extremely difficult winter. I was so anxious that I lost twenty-five pounds. I didn't sleep for months and eventually, after the help of a wonderful psychiatrist, found out that I had obsessive-compulsive disorder (OCD). It took months for me to feel normal again. I remember going with Alexa to visit Tina. I was sitting on the edge of her hospital bed, and it felt like the room was spinning. My own excruciating anxiety was heightened by seeing my beloved sister in this ward. She was quiet, and so extremely low.

The psychiatrist determined that Tina's depression was so severe that he recommended electric convulsive therapy (ECT). Experts disagree about its safety and effectiveness, but for some people with debilitating depression, ECT shocks the brain into a new pattern. The process involves giving an electric current to the brain which in turn triggers a seizure.

The procedure has come a long way since the film *One Flew Over the Cuckoo's Nest* (1975), which shows the Jack Nicholson character foaming at the mouth after shock therapy. Patients do not feel the seizure as they are under monitored sedation. There is unilateral and bilateral ECT. In unilateral ECT, a node is placed on one side of the brain, and bilateral nodes are placed on both sides.

My brother Spencer, who is a psychiatrist, urged Tina not to get the bilateral ECT, as it can cause severe memory loss, but Tina and Bill chose it anyway because Tina wanted the most powerful treatment she was offered. Over a period of about four months, Tina had twenty to thirty ECT treatments. The treatments were helpful. For periods of time, she was able to function normally again. She could get up, accomplish tasks, and interact with her family. The girls were eleven and sixteen at the time. Sadly, her memory was truly affected. Every time I brought up a childhood or college memory, she had no idea what I was referring to. She would say, "Sorry, Ing. My memory is so bad now." Even though that made me sad, I was glad she was able to function.

In the spring of 2012, Tina returned to the Caymans. She did not tell Sally about the ECT treatments though she did tell her that she had suffered a terrible depression over the summer and fall. Sally recalls Tina describing it as falling into a deep, black hole, with walls so high no light could get through and walls so smooth she couldn't grasp onto anything to crawl up and out. Sally also vividly remembers Tina telling her that if she ever fell into that place again, she was done. She wouldn't try to fight her way out again. Tina's behavior at the Caymans in 2012 was worrisome enough to Sally that she called Bill at the end of the week to say she thought there was something wrong with Tina, "something serious," but he assured Sally that Tina was fine. Before Sally extended an invitation for the Spring of 2013, she reached out to Bill again, saying that she was very worried about Tina's depression and that perhaps she shouldn't come. Again, Bill assured her that everything was fine, and in May, 2013, Tina returned to the Caymans.

As Sally later told me, everything was just off. The first day Tina stumbled on the beach and when she entered the water, she told Sally she didn't remember how to swim. At one point, one of the women introduced a vacation "rule" that no one was allowed to apologize for their bodies. Tina didn't like this, as her humor at this point was at the expense of her mind, her body, and her financial situation. She shared a room with a Dartmouth friend named Valerie, who grew concerned about Tina's behaviors. Tina slept a lot, used Valerie's toothbrush, and didn't flush the toilet. (Tina didn't always flush after peeing, and it annoyed Valerie.) They ended up having an argument, and late one night, Tina called the manager of the condos and asked if there was a free unit. The manager called Sally who tracked down Tina and told her how rude it was for her to leave without telling anyone.

Sally was seeing a pattern that started in 2011. Tina's behaviors were erratic. As Sally says, "Her tone changed from ironic and funny to something I couldn't name, but that felt different and markedly not funny." Tina's marriage was falling part. Sally was getting divorced, but she hadn't told anyone on the trip because they hadn't told their two girls yet. She wanted so badly to have the support of her dearest friends on that trip. Instead, she had to deal with Tina's illness and emotional spiral; it was just too much. Again, Sally was so worried she called Bill. He told her again that Tina was fine. This is the email that Tina wrote to Sally in September of 2013. You can see her humor but also her darkness and her poor self-image, a symptom of borderline personality disorder:

> It's your disgusting, flabby, poor, alleged toothbrush
> stealing erstwhile ex-friend Tina, here. The one who has bad
> bathroom habits, who sent your parents flowers they hated
> for years (still blushing about that one), the walking fart
> no one would share a bed with. That Tina. BTW the $300
> I told you my father gave Sophie for watching my wildly
> demented mom for three hours was actually only $100. I
> was incorrect. How the rest of you could boast so endlessly

about college tuitions being covered by parents and at the same time go ape shit over what happened to be a $100 payment to a grandchild whose grandparents DO NOT pay her college tuition I will never understand. Is it a matter of not deserving what the rest of you do? Maybe someday you can help me do the math. Enough about that. I know that you and your friends (with the exception of Valerie) are wonderful, fine people. You just are not good for me, el-dis-gusterus. I will always adore you.

Tina's email reminds me of many I received from her during her last years. Her emails could be venomous and as part of her stonewalling strategy, I wasn't allowed to defend myself. It should be noted that our parents did pay for Tina's two girls to attend private school, grades K-12. Hence, her comment about grandparents not paying for college was ridiculous. She would fling insults and barbs when it suited her but often refused to see the bigger picture. Later in the email, Tina told Sally she would be in Chicago and asked her if they could meet for coffee. Sally was hurt. She wasn't ready to see Tina yet; the memory of her leaving the vacation mid-week and slamming her best friends was too raw.

Almost a year later, Tina returned to the Caymans by herself. She had met a woman there who said she could rent her home. When she arrived and opened the home, apparently, there were green iguanas everywhere. Here is her email to Bill:

Smooth trip takes longer to get to Lopez than here and arrived safely at the Discovery Point Club. This next part is unbelievable so feel free to call me a liar. I arrived at the cute little beach club studio to discover that a LARGE number of LARGE lizards and iguanas had already booked the place. My screams of fear and distress and panic resulted in many people rushing to help, including the island's EMT. My heart was pounding out of my chest and

I was hyperventilating and actually was on an oxygen tank for a while. The locals scratched their heads and said: "No wonder Missus Violy has such a hard time renting this place!?" **They have me in unit 29 for tonight. The number here is 345-945-5159. I cannot receive texts, but finally figured out how to get** online. Calling here is wicked expensive so we should avoid it. They say they are in touch with Missus Violy and that they will clear the place of the iguanas/lizards and do a deep clean to the unit. I say that I will not stay in a place that is knee-deep in iguana shit and eggs and that they need me to find me a new condo, even if CIA and NASA do the deep cleaning. They are being very helpful. All to say I may be back tomorrow. I will keep you posted.

I'm not saying the iguana story isn't true, but Tina had started a pattern of telling lies to cover up bad behavior. Bill said to me, "Tina has become a chronic liar." As a family, we were swimming in her sickness. She was drowning, and we knew it.

In the spring of 2014, six months before she died, Tina arranged to have lunch with Sally. She hoped to regain her friendship with Sally. She gave her one of the silver necklaces she had worn on every trip, knowing that Sally had always admired it. Perhaps Tina knew that this was the last time they would ever see each other. Like me, Sally feels that she missed something that day though she couldn't have known. She misses Tina terribly.

One aspect I have trouble with is that Sally's warnings to Bill seemed to go unheeded. When Tina became ill, Bill was really the only one parenting the girls. Also, the day Tina was admitted to Swedish, Bill was supposed to start a new job. But with Tina in the hospital and two children at home, he had to delay the start. He was overwhelmed. I just wish that Bill had reached out to me, Dad, Alexa, and Spencer more and had asked us to help. I don't know if it was pride, or if Tina had asked him not to involve her family. After Tina died, I called Sally and asked, "Why didn't you call me when Tina's behavior in the Caymans became so strange?" She responded, "Ingrid, I should have."

# CHAPTER 20

# Alexa and Mark's Wedding

Alexa and her husband Mark were married at my in-laws' property in September of 2013. My mother-in-law, Sally, and her friend Jill planned and hosted weddings on their property for many years. Their home was at the center of the farm and a fifty-yard walk for my family. My father-in-law was a former judge, and he officiated at many weddings, including Alexa's and ours. Tina's behavior was very troubling on their wedding day. Tina and I were Alexa's co-maids of honor. Having that honor, we were supposed to be there for hair and makeup with all the bridesmaids and to help Alexa put on her wedding dress. About fifteen minutes into the makeup time, my cousin Chelsea asked, "Hey, Ing. Where is Tina?" "I have no idea," I said. Not until the moment Alexa had her dress on did Tina arrive. As she walked into the bedroom, she looked like she was swaying a little. Her speech was slow, and I knew from experience that she was loaded up on anti-anxiety meds. I wondered how she had driven the thirty minutes from their home.

The wedding was spectacular; Alexa has the same creative gene Tina had. The wedding theme was "farm chic," and no detail went unnoticed. As usual I was worried about Tina the entire evening. At dinner, our uncle Joe sat at the same table with Eric, me, and our kids. I remember him asking, "Ingrid, what is wrong with Tina? She seems like she's on something." I replied, "She is struggling, Joe. She has a lot of anxieties right now." Like many times before, my heart broke for her. As a family, we were supposed to be celebrating one of the happiest days of Alexa's life. Yet Tina was suffering, and she couldn't hide it. It must have been really hard for her to attend a wedding when her own life seemed so heavy.

# CHAPTER 21

# The Intervention

In the early winter of 2014, Tina's behavior became frightening. She and Bill were in the process of separating, heading toward divorce. They needed money, so they had to sell their beautiful home. Tina rented a small home in the Madison Park neighborhood. With her talent for decorating, she made that small rental home as fabulous as possible, full of color, textures and family pictures. Sophie was in college in Chicago at this time, and Sylvie was a freshman in high school. Bill rented a home in north Seattle, near Sylvie's school. Sylvie spent her time between Tina and Bill's homes, but Tina essentially had stopped being a mother. She called me one night and told me that Sylvie wanted her to make her dinner. I asked, "What's strange about that?" Her response was, "Well, I like to eat earlier and don't want to make another meal when she wants to eat." Consequently, Sylvie chose to live almost exclusively with Bill. She also didn't want to be in a car with Tina because Tina had started to get in car accidents, multiple fender benders. She had ten car accidents in 2014. One of her last email messages to Bill was to inform him that their insurance company had dropped them.

One night, our family was at a restaurant. Spence noticed Tina was drinking a lot of vodka at dinner. He said, "Tina, you should not be mixing alcohol with all of your medications, including Xanax and the antidepressants." She looked at Spencer and said, "Well, the other alternative is just to kill myself." The conversation was between them. He told me about it later. When we were leaving the restaurant, Spence noticed a big dent in her car. "Tina, what happened?" She said, "Oh, the garage door came off of its tracks and fell on my car." Another lie. It had been from one of her accidents.

Soon after this dinner, I instigated a family intervention. If her behaviors continued, she was either going to kill someone or be killed in her car, among other horrible scenarios. We needed Tina to agree to a rehabilitation facility. With the help of family and close friends, I researched facilities in the western US. As a family, we agreed on Alta Mira in Sausalito, California. I also found a wonderful woman who leads interventions. She was in her sixties and had orchestrated hundreds of family interventions in the Seattle region. It is a very emotional process. There are meetings beforehand among family members. Everyone has to agree to their role. We all wrote letters of compassion, concern, and love to be read to Tina on that day. We decided to hold the meeting at Alexa's home in Seattle in the summer of 2014. I think it was disguised as a family meeting to talk about financial matters. Minutes before Tina was to arrive, Alexa had a minor panic attack. She said, "Ing, I can't do this, not here." She didn't want her home to be associated with bad memories for Tina. I responded, "It will be OK. We have to do this to save Tina's life."

Soon after Tina arrived, the interventionist began the meeting. She was kind and gentle and told Tina why we really gathered. Tina's tears flowed, and she said, "I've been waiting until Sylvie turns eighteen until I kill myself." Sylvie was fifteen and a half at the time. Several family members read their letters. There were many tears and hugs and important, painful issues were discussed. The process of an intervention is that if the person agrees to go to rehab, they leave within hours. Dad and Spence accompanied her to California. First, they went to her home so she could pack. The experience was emotionally draining for all of us, but we were all incredibly hopeful that Tina could get clean and begin a new chapter. I was so optimistic that rehab would be a new start for her, an opportunity to rediscover all of her wonderful talents.

# Alta Mira

Alta Mira did not end up being the answer we were all hoping for. At first, it seemed like Tina was grateful to be there and to meet other people who were struggling with addiction. We all received letters from her. I wrote her the day after she left to apologize for being so judgmental and to let her know that I really just wanted to see her come back to life. Her letter back to me was kind and loving.

When she was able to have her first visitors, Dad, Alexa, and I flew to San Francisco. In the taxi on the way from SFO to Sausalito, I was nervous to see her and perhaps too hopeful there had been great changes. The three of us waited in the lobby for her. When she came down the stairs and saw us, she smiled. We gave her big bear hugs and kisses, and we took her out to lunch. At lunch, she didn't say much except that that detoxing from Xanax or diazepam was incredibly hard for her. Remember, she was taking up to 300 mg per day. She told us that after heroin, it's the worst drug to recover from because it "rests in one's nervous system." That is not actually true; Xanax only stays in a person's system for a brief time. But withdrawal from Xanax can be severe, even life-threatening, so in that respect, it's nearly as bad as heroin.

After lunch, we had a tour of the facilities. There was such a sense of sadness there. You could feel the heaviness of the place. There was a big deck with a beautiful view of San Francisco Bay. There were ashtrays everywhere, as many recovering addicts turn to smoking. Tina had befriended a nice woman who had checked herself into rehab after realizing she was drinking two bottles of Chardonnay every night. She said, "It's really nice to meet some of Tina's family. She talks about all of you a lot." There was another woman sitting on the deck whose son was spending his fourth time in a rehab facility, heroin being his drug of choice.

The policy was that everyone had a roommate, though they made an exception for Tina because she was so insistent. She told us, "I cannot share a room with anyone. I can't stand the smell of cigarettes on people's clothes in my room, and I can't stand any degree of snoring." Sitting on that deck with Tina, Dad, and Alexa, I had two distinct thoughts. First, our mom had been in a facility very similar to this one. Second, Tina was just going through the motions. It didn't really seem like she wanted to get better. We were only there for half a day, and then visiting hours were over. When we left, I felt very uneasy. Throughout July and August, there were rumblings that Tina hated it there, hated her team of therapists and doctors, and just wanted to come home.

In September of 2014, Alta Mira hosted a family weekend where patients and their loved ones went through intensive therapy sessions together for three days. Dad, Bill, Spencer, Alexa, and I were all prepped to fly to Sausalito. The day before we were scheduled to leave, Tina called 911 from Alta Mira and said she was suicidal; she was taken by ambulance to Marin County General. After she was discharged from the hospital, she didn't return to Alta Mira; she took a cab to SFO and flew back to Seattle. Her friend Linda Hoedemaker took her to her own home. I was furious. How were we supposed to have a family weekend with the patient who wasn't there?! I was leaving children and responsibilities at home. Regardless, we all decided to go and forge ahead without Tina, so we could learn.

The experts running the weekend said they had never worked with a family whose loved one wasn't present. We all learned a lot about addiction, love, grace, and compassion but also about enabling loved ones to continue down bad paths. Enablers allow people to make bad choices by turning a blind eye. It's easier to say yes than it is to say no. Bill struggled with this more than we did. Their marriage was disintegrating, and he was also the only one parenting Sophie and Sylvie. There's only so much a partner can do.

At one point, the four of us met with Tina's primary psychologist. She was a petite, very pretty brunette. I asked her a question: "Tina said she is experiencing terrible withdrawals from the benzos, that her body constantly feels like it's buzzing all the time. Why would her body be buzzing?" She replied, "Well, that's Tina's perception of how she is feeling." I asked, "What does that mean?" She said, "Tina has a perception about her recovery from alcohol and drug abuse that is uniquely attached to Tina, whether it's true or not." I continued, "Do a lot of recovering addicts have these sensations?" When the psychologist gave me a smug look and didn't choose to continue with the topic, I realized why Tina didn't like her.

I'll never forget the last session on the final day. The therapist asked us to pretend we were talking to Tina, and she filled in as if she was Tina. When it was my turn she asked, "Ingrid, what would you most like to say to me?" I burst into tears and said, "I am afraid you are going to kill yourself." Sitting in the airport waiting to board our flight home, I remember thinking how the Bay Area had held so many strong, loving memories of us together, and now the region only held sadness for me. I have several close friends who live in the Bay Area, and I just don't like visiting there anymore.

After I returned home, I went to visit Tina at Linda's home, the first of many heart-wrenching visits that fall. Tina was staying in Linda's son's room. Linda's daughter Ivaly was still in high school and was there as well. I said, "Tina, we all learned a lot at Alta Mira, but we really wish you had been there." She said, "I just couldn't be there." She was sitting in bed, so distant from me, so sad. I could feel there was anger toward me, but she never said so. During that time, Tina could only eat yogurt and string cheese and the protein drink Ensure. Again, she said her whole body was emitting electrical shots, and nothing seemed appealing or edible. After she had been there for a week, I told Linda I would take her to my home. She stayed in our guestroom. The only smile I saw was when our daughter Hazel came into her room and hugged her. I wanted to be helpful so badly, but she was so very low. When I asked her about suicidal thoughts, she said, "Yes, I do want to kill myself."

One morning instead of bringing yogurt to her room, I said, "Please come to the kitchen and eat with me." Begrudgingly she came in and sat in silence. I remember thinking, "Where has Tina gone? Where is that spark, that intelligence, that humor?" I couldn't have her stay with us. I think I was terrified that she would do something in our home. She only stayed with me for two nights. Then she went back to Linda's and eventually was able to move back to her own home. I feel intense guilt for having her leave my house. Sometimes I sleep in that guest room, and when I do, I always think about when Tina was there, feeling that intense depression, and the decision I made to have her leave. I am not justifying it, but I was so emotionally exhausted from the time at Alta Mira that I think I needed a break from constantly worrying about her every minute. I had also developed a very defeatist attitude. If she wouldn't try to help herself, how could I help her?

# CHAPTER 23

# Preparing to End Her Life

Without alcohol and Xanax to mask her pain, Tina had lost her will to live. She had used both as a crutch for such a long time. She couldn't see a way forward. I visited her once or twice a week to bring her a coffee and some groceries. One day, I brought her flowers and she said, "Why would you bring me flowers?" I said, "Um, because I love you." She said, "Why would anybody love me after everything I have done?" I asked her several times, "Are you suicidal?" When she would say "Yes," I'd say, "Well, I am supposed to call 911." Her response: "Then what? They will take me to an ER, and I am not allowed any type of sedative because I am an addict." Every time I visited, I cried on my way home. I couldn't get her to talk, at least not very much. Dad and Bill were trying as well. Bill spent a lot of time with her. She wanted to move back in with him and Sylvie. Bill didn't want to expose Sylvie to Tina's severe depression, especially after the trauma of living with her before the intervention and the time away at rehab. Sylvie was only fifteen at the time, trying to navigate high school with a very ill mother.

After about a month of this, I told Dad and Bill that we needed another approach. I wanted her to go the Menninger Clinic in Houston, one of the top psychiatric programs in the nation. Dad, Bill, and I met with her at her home. After we suggested Menninger, Tina said, "I do not want to go away again to another type of facility. I just have to come back eventually and try and start over a second time." I said, "We are so worried about you. You are so depressed. You hardly ever talk." She refused. I was so frustrated that I stood up and walked out. I slammed her door when I left, something she pointed out in her last letters to us. When someone you love so deeply starts talking this way, it is incredibly painful, stressful, and hopeless. Tina was slipping away. She and I had once made mud pies together, gone to college together, and shared parenting; she wasn't that Tina anymore. My heart was broken because her heart was shattered.

As the fall progressed, she was getting weekly DBT treatment in Seattle. DBT stands for Dialectical Behavioral Therapy. DBT was developed by a psychological researcher at the University of Washington named Marsha Linehan. Originally, Doctor Linehan was using DBT to treat borderline personality disorder as well as individuals who are chronically suicidal. According to Wikipedia, "the chronically suicidal patients she studied had been raised in profoundly invalidating environments."

When a patient is involved in DBT training, the first step is to learn about the triggers that lead to their reactive states. The second step is for the therapist and the patient to discover which coping skills can be used to avoid undesirable reactions. Today DBT is used to treat multiple illnesses such as depression, addiction, PTSD, and mood disorders. I actually think that Tina was finally involved in the right type of therapy for her. However, she had lost too much of her former life to see a path forward. Between childhood, severe depression, alcohol, Xanax, financial and marital decline, the mountain must have seemed insurmountable.

In mid-December, Tina, Alexa, Hazel, and our cousin Chelsea met for lunch near Tina's home. When she walked into the restaurant, she had cut her long hair into a short bob. I said, "It looks cute!" She replied, "Well, nobody looks at me anymore, so I cut it off." Looking back, I wonder if she cut it to make the end-of-life process easier. On December 22nd, we had a large gathering at my uncle Joe's home with extended family members from Mom's side. When it was time to eat, Tina got her dinner in the buffet line. She didn't see her name on a place card on the table, so she went and sat in a chair in the living room. I said, "Tina there's a place for you here at the table." She came back slowly, ate, and didn't say much to anyone.

After dinner, Tina and my father were sitting near the fire. I went over to sit with them. They were talking about a financial matter. Dad asked her a question about some kind of payment, and she said, "Do whatever you think is best. I don't care." She also apologized for getting angry with me at the aforementioned lunch. Much later, I realized she knew she would never see me again. After she died, Bill found the receipt for the handguns she had purchased, as well as the information about the gun course she had taken a month prior. She had hidden those receipts in a basket underneath her bed. The day of the party she had purchased the guns. She had known it was the last time she was going to see most of her family. As Bill said, "That evening had to have been so hard for her."

Several days before her death, she was preparing her life to say goodbye. She was writing letters, making piles of scarves and jewelry and mementos to leave for the special women in her life, but not for me. Her daughter Sophie and Sophie's girlfriend Laura were flying to Seattle from Chicago. Tina told Sophie she couldn't come to her home because she had had a break-in, and the police were investigating. Of course, she couldn't let her daughter see what she was doing. When she did see Sophie, she handed over her ATM card. In retrospect, we know that all of these actions were signs of what she was planning, but we all missed them.

# CHAPTER 24

# New Year's Eve 2014

In the late afternoon of New Year's Eve, Tina sent Bill a text, saying, "My car will be at the Four Seasons Hotel in Seattle." Feeling alarmed, he contacted our dad. Dad had also received a strange email with a finality to it. Soon after that my father called the hotel manager and said, "My daughter is staying there, and we are concerned about a possible suicide attempt." Tina had checked in two days prior. She had a massage, sent laundry out for cleaning, and had drunk a little alcohol from the minibar. Sometime between 4:30 and 5:00 p.m., she shot herself in the head. Apparently, there were two handguns in her room. None of us will ever know why she purchased two guns. Perhaps she wanted a backup just in case the first gun didn't fire. Apparently, there are a lot of suicides on New Year's Eve. People can't imagine starting another year feeling their pain. I know about when she died because, in her way, she did say goodbye.

That afternoon in Palm Desert, Hazel wanted to play tennis with me. It was windy and getting dark, but I said OK. We went to the courts and turned on the lights. It was very gusty, but as we were hitting the ball, the wind suddenly stopped, and it became quiet. Then a large flock of birds flew directly over the court. I stopped and asked, "Hazel, did you feel that? The wind stopping?" She said, "No, but a bird just flew over and pooped right next to me." That was Tina's mistake. I am sure the poop was meant for me. She was leaving the earth and saying goodbye.

After Eric told me about Tina, Henry, George and Hazel came into our bedroom, all crying. They held me tight and kept saying, "Oh Mama. Oh Mama." They loved their aunt "Tee Ta." When I called my father, who told me all the details, I lost it. It was like an out-of-body experience. A few minutes after Eric told me, I thought, "I never ever have to worry about her again." My brain was a jumble of conflicting thoughts, the predominant one being grief. I called Alaska Airlines that night and got all of us on an 8:00 a.m. flight home. That night, I crawled into Hazel's bed to sleep with her, but I couldn't sleep, so I moved out to the couch. I roamed around and maybe slept a couple hours. Our good friend picked us up the next morning, to take us to the airport. After security, I went to Starbucks. I saw Cherise, a friend of mine, but I turned around so she wouldn't see me. I just couldn't talk to anyone. On the plane, I was crying, and the friend saw me as she was walking to her seat. (A few days later, Cherise reached out and said, "Ing, I am so sorry. It makes sense to me now.") I cried for a while on Eric's shoulder and said, "I am never going to see her again, am I?" From the airport, we drove directly to Bill's house. Sophie and Sylvie had set up a little shrine to their mama, with photos and a candle burning. Sylvie was up in her room. I went into her room, crawled into bed with her, held her, and said, "Sylvie, you will never, ever go through anything harder than this." Bill told me that Sylvie kept calling Tina's cell phone and leaving Tina messages. I still want to cry when I think about this. She had just turned sixteen on December 23. Sophie's girlfriend Laura Sachin stayed with Sophie, Sylvie, and Bill for three weeks after Tina died. I will forever be grateful for her. She took care of them. She was only twenty-two but had the heart and compassion of a much older person. If you should ever read this book, Laura, thank you, thank you. What a gift.

Tina and Bill on their
wedding day

In front of our home

Tina and Sophie

Tina and Sylvie

Tina and Sylvie

Messing Family          Page and Tina

Aunt Maggie's wedding, April 2000    Spa day before Alexa's wedding

Tina, Ingrid, Dad Christmas Eve    Cousins Hazel, Sylvie, Anabelle

Tina's jewelry

# Part Three: My Road Back (2015–present)

# CHAPTER 25

# How Do I Move Forward?

I took me almost two years to stop replaying the last moments of Tina's life. With OCD, I tend to obsess over images. I just kept replaying the last minutes, the gun to her head, and I know this sounds weird, but also how she had the courage to pull the trigger. Relentlessly, I have asked myself, "What if I had called her right before it happened? Would she have answered, or talked to me?" Most women do not use guns to end their lives. It is too violent. Tina was very smart and researched the most effective way to end her life. One of the eeriest parts of the story is that my uncle Joe was having a drink at the Four Seasons with a friend that night. He said there were several police officers and ambulances, and he later found out it was because of Tina. I also wonder, if she had run into Joe that night in the hotel, would she have changed her mind?

I felt such pain, anger and suffocating guilt after she died. Why couldn't I stop her? Ironically, most people who die by suicide do not discuss it beforehand. I suppose I thought, if she's talking about it so much, she probably won't do it? How did we miss the preparation? What if? What if? What if? I obsessed over calling the Seattle Police Department to see if I could speak with the officers who found her, but I never called.

Fortunately, I have a wonderful therapist. I hadn't seen Dr. Blake in a while though I went back after Tina's demise. I remember her saying, "When someone plans to end their life, they will do it. There is nothing you could have done differently." Yet, the guilt continued. My father and Bill went to see her body before she was cremated. They asked me to come.

I couldn't do it. I wonder if seeing her body would have given me some peace. I'll never know. Tina did leave behind letters, one for Dad, one for Bill, one for Sophie and Sylvie. In her letters to her daughters, she told them that she did not want them to have a mother with mental illness. Of course, she also expressed her deep love to them. Her letter to Dad was angry, sad, accusatory. That must have been heartbreaking for him. He did so much for her and tried everything he knew to help her. Dad let me read her letter, and after I did, he shredded it. In her letter, Tina said, "I do not want Sophie and Sylvie to have anything to do with the Jarvis family. My front door will never be the same after Ingrid slammed it." She left behind favorite scarves and jewelry for her best friends, for Alexa, and for our dear cousin Chelsea. Nothing for me. Over the years, I have realized that the three people in her life trying the hardest to get her well were the three she showed disdain for: Bill, Dad, and me.

Linda Hoedemaker wrote this to me: "The thing I wanted to tell you after we talked is that while I provided support to Tina at the end, you supported her for years and years before that. If she could back up now and have perspective on her life, she would name you as her biggest love/supporter. I was always envious of your relationship. Even though there was lots of yelling and drama, under all that was a precious connection."

I was also so angry with Tina for leaving us. Part of the anger was that I never was, nor ever desired to be the oldest child. I was perfectly happy in my role in our family as the middle child. It always suited me. Suddenly, I was the oldest child, and with that, came responsibilities. One of those responsibilities was helping to coordinate a memorial. After her death, my family disagreed about how we should honor Tina. Dad, Alexa, Spencer, and I wanted to have a very small family gathering and say goodbye. Bill insisted that we hold a memorial. The service was primarily for Sophie and Sylvie, but also for the many, many others who had held Tina in high regard and were shocked and grieving her death. We eventually agreed, and Bill was right. It was absolutely the right decision. I am grateful to Bill for being persistent.

# CHAPTER 26

# The Memorial

The spectacular Chihuly Garden and Glass Museum in downtown Seattle is owned by the Wright family, old friends of ours. Howard S. Wright, Sr., and my father worked together for many years. Howard's son, Jeff Wright, graciously offered the Chihuly Museum for the memorial, free of charge. Tina's Lakeside classmate Kathy Jobs Gerke was the Director of Sales at the Chihuly. She helped our family with the entire service, and she could not have been more empathetic or gracious. The memorial was held in the Glasshouse. There were 450 people there that day, January 17, 2015, the day after what would have been Tina's fifty-second birthday. The tribute was beautiful. It was raining outside and Pierre's sister, Natalie, said, "Ingrid, the rain was like everyone's tears streaming down the outside." Bill, Sophie, Page, and I spoke. Killian Noe, the director of the Recovery Café gave the eulogy, and our friends John and Jim Sangster played their guitars and sang a song. After the service, there was a long line of people wanting to hug me. It's not that my family members weren't hugged as well, but so many people there were from our high school, college, and beyond. We were Tina and Ingrid, Ingrid and Tina. They knew, and although they didn't say it aloud, they were thinking, "What is Ingrid going to do without Tina?"

For the winter months, I pretty much sat in my bed, cried, talked to family and close friends, and watched Netflix. Eric never pushed me. He let me grieve the way that I needed to, without judgment. Flowers and meals poured in from family and friends. A local florist reached out and said, "I am so sorry." Our address just kept popping up on his screen. I received nearly ninety notes from family, long-time friends, high school friends, college friends, neighbors, and co-workers. Recently, I pulled the notes out of the bottom drawer of my desk and reread them. Here are some of the adjectives and phrases people used to describe Tina: beautiful (so many times), brilliant, intelligent, whip-smart, complex, powerful, witty, funny, compassionate, kind, empathetic, a great storyteller, with a vibrant smile, and a contagious laugh.

# CHAPTER 27

# Signs

For about three weeks after Tina died, I found pennies everywhere. A penny near my bathroom sink, pennies in the kitchen, a penny on my car floor mat, pennies in my pocket. My friend Toni had recently lost her mom. I called her and asked, "Toni, did you find pennies everywhere after your mom died?" She emphatically replied, "Yes!" I had to google it. The expression "pennies from heaven" is based on the belief that deceased loved ones are watching you, and that you are valued and loved. It's a thing! There was some solace in that. Because Tina didn't leave behind any of her jewelry, a note, or a kind word, I'd like to think it was her way of saying she loved me. I was missing Tina so much that it physically hurt.

One day I drove to the mall in Bellevue, which is near where we grew up. I pulled into the parking spot, and an intense wave of grief washed over me. Tears flowed, and I needed to call someone who knew her well. I called Jessica. She picked up, soothed me. Those moments helped me to heal. About three months after Tina's death, I hired a medium. This woman was moving her offices, but she said she could do it over the phone. She warned me that the person I was hoping to know about might not be the one who would "come to her." I told her that was OK. We spoke for an hour. She started by saying, "I am seeing a point on the map in the Midwest, and an older woman who loved to bake. She has been waiting for her." My dad's mother Ellen Helsell was from Iowa. She died in 1980. The medium referenced the two types of cookies she most loved to bake.

She continued, saying that the process was more painful than she thought it would be, which I inferred to mean that the suicide wasn't as she thought. She was definitely channeling Tina as her visions increased. She said Tina had found a sense of peace at the top of the mountain and hadn't felt so free in a long, long time. The psychic kept seeing two intertwined S's and asked me what I thought that meant. I said, "I am guessing her daughters Sophie and Sylvie." She went on to say that Tina would like me to watch out for them as they grow up. Whether this was true or not, it gave me great comfort, given the parting letter Tina wrote. She also referenced a man in her life, who had been very, very difficult for her. This woman had never met me, didn't know anything about my family, Tina, or the way she died. I had done some research on the internet, and she came highly recommended. That conversation gave me a bit of peace.

This past spring, I received a sign and undoubtedly, this one has been the most poignant. I have been a tennis player my whole life and competed locally for thirteen years, from age thirty-two to forty-five. I took a five-year hiatus from the sport and resumed again in my late forties but very casually, no competition. In April, I was playing in my club's Ladies Day Thursday morning session, which is a weekly gathering of women who want to play with friends and for fun. On one Thursday morning, my partner was a beautiful, petite brunette with a huge smile. We introduced ourselves, and she said, "Hi, my name is Tina." I almost choked up because in some ways, she reminded me of my Tina. She has dark hair and big brown eyes. It was the first time I had met another Tina that I was doing something with. After the match, Tina asked, "Ingrid, would you have any interest in joining my USTA team? Matches have started, but we could use another player." I said, "Maybe. Let me think about it." About a week later, I joined Tina's team, and it was one of the best decisions I made. Every single woman on the team is kind, smart, athletic, fun, and eager to be a better tennis player. I was the oldest woman on the team and have played on many, many teams. There was an enthusiasm and general loveliness about this team that I hadn't experienced, at least not since my mid-thirties.

Soon after I joined, I was playing with some women from the team, to meet others and practice. After we played, Tina and I walked out to the lobby. We were standing in the corner, talking. Her eyes welled up with tears, and she said, "Ingrid, I think we have something in common."

I asked, "What's that?" Tina replied, "My brother took his life five years ago. He was thirty-five." I couldn't believe it. Her name was Tina and she was also a suicide survivor. Tina added, "Tennis was my therapy after he died."

Tina is forty-four. Although she started learning tennis late in life, she is an incredible player. She has a wicked forehand, a very strong serve, and is a force at the net. She isn't very tall, but she poaches on every shot she can, and she gets a lot of balls. For my first match, Tina and I were paired up. She played the forehand side, me on the backhand, both of our strengths. We played against two women, and their team was at the top of the leader board in our division. We lost, but it didn't matter. I was happy playing a sport with a lovely, kind Tina. Our team made it to the playoffs, and we were paired up again. We played a tough match against tough opponents and ended up with a win. When our opponent hit their last shot to give us the win, I ran over to Tina and gave her a big hug. She was probably a bit surprised.

Meeting Tina was a sign for me, a sign that perhaps my Tina is watching over me. At least, that's what I choose to believe. I don't know if it's because I look for signs or they actually do present themselves. Either way, I want signs to keep happening because it's my way of feeling close to my sister again.

Fall used to be my favorite time of year. The kids went back to school, and I had more freedom. September was always a reset. I started to exercise more, lose the chips and cocktail weight from the summer. Also, September is glorious in Seattle. Late summer warmth is tinged by emerging fall colors. Since Tina's death it is no longer my favorite season. Every September, I am reminded of Tina's last months, fraught with tremendous pain for her while I felt helpless to do anything to help. The holidays are tougher too. There is always a visceral absence in the Helsell gatherings. Tina never met Mark and Alexa's precious children, Grace and Bo, who are six and three now. Alexa and I always talk about how much she would have loved them. Grace reminds me of Tina. She is smart, headstrong, creative. My heart hurts for Lex because I know how much she would have loved her oldest sister to be a part of her family's life. And they share a birthday. While New Year's is always painful for me, January 16 is harder for Lex. At least Spencer and I have many memories of get-togethers with our children, and of Tina cherishing each niece and nephew.

# CHAPTER 28

# Forefront

Shortly after Tina died, a woman named Katie Simmons called me. Her daughter was a friend of Sylvie's. Katie was so kind and loving toward Bill and Sylvie. (Sophie was in college at the time.) Katie had lost her brother to suicide, and she was working for an organization called Forefront, a suicide prevention organization. She was raising money and awareness. She sent me, Dad, Bill, Spence, and Alexa a beautiful care package, with a candle, poetry, and books about suicide and loss. It was a healing box. Katie brought the package as part of the Forefront Cares program. The survivor support program is now with Crisis Connections and is called CC Cares.

Forefront is an organization started in Seattle in 2013 by Jennifer Stuber PhD and Sue Eastgard, M.S.W. Jennifer lost her husband, Matt, to suicide in 2011 when their children were one and five. Jen is a professor in the School of Social Work at the University of Washington. Sue Eastgard is a nationally renowned prevention expert for youth suicide. Forefront was their brainchild, an organization that focuses solely on suicide awareness, education, and prevention.

According to the National Institute of Mental Health, in 2018, suicide was the tenth leading cause of death in the United States, with forty-eight thousand souls lost. It was the second leading cause of death for ages ten through thirty-four and the fifth leading cause for ages thirty-five through fifty-four. There were two and a half more times the numbers of suicides than homicides. Suicide rates are the highest in the Rocky Mountain states and the western US. Among my friends and acquaintances, I know of eight suicides of people ages sixteen through fifty-five.

The work Jenn, Sue, and their team have done is truly remarkable. Together they have worked on eleven state laws in the state of Washington. One of these laws is that all behavioral health providers and health care workers are required to have training in how to identify and intervene with a person who may be at-risk for suicide. This law is the first of its kind in the country. Forefront has established programs for fifty high schools. The entire teaching staff and student body are trained to be able to talk about depression, mental health, and suicide. Most recently they advocated for the HB 1477 bill, an incredibly significant piece of legislation that finally passed. As a result, there will be significant reforms to the behavioral health crisis system in Washington State providing robust implementation of the national 9-8-8-number. This is a much-needed expansion. Instead of phoning the police or emergency services, a person in need will get access to suicide prevention services, mental health, and substance abuse care.

A year after Tina died, in January of 2016, we orchestrated a lecture at Seattle Children's Hospital and Medical Center with the help of the members of my wonderful Seattle Children's Guild. In collaboration with Forefront, we raised money for Seattle Children's Hospital to provide families with lockboxes to lock up firearms and potentially harmful pills. We had experts from Forefront speak about suicide, prevention, and general knowledge. We also had a psychiatrist give a talk about dialectical behavioral theory, the method Tina was learning before she died. Tina was a founding member of our guild and a very active member. Several years ago, the guild members wanted to change our name to the "Tina Helsell Guild." They will never know how honored I felt when they announced this.

We suicide-loss survivors belong to a "club" that we never wanted to join. We are united by our grief for the missing friend or family member and by our unanswered questions. We have felt the judgment of those who view suicide as a crime and the worst thing one can do to a family. I definitely received that vibe from certain family members and friends. I gained much insight into the ignorance surrounding suicide from Forefront. Jenn Stuber really dislikes the term "committed suicide" because it suggests a crime. She prefers to use the term, "died by suicide." Also, people don't take their lives because they want to leave this earth. They take their lives because THEY WANT TO END THEIR PAIN. About two years after Tina's death, I was trained to be a peer mentor for Forefront, to guide people through the loss of suicide. I was a mentor for about a year but began to find it too painful. I just wasn't ready; I needed much more time to heal myself.

Perhaps this isn't true for all people who are loss survivors, but I really, really love it when people talk about Tina. Most people avoid the topic because they think it will hurt me, but it has the opposite effect. When people talk about Tina, I'm reminded that she lived, was loved, had an impact, and left someone with a wonderful memory, joke, experience. I remember the little things. After she poured coffee, she would always lick the top of the mug before taking a sip. She had a special zipper on her pillow that she always liked to touch before sleep. These memories give me a sense of peace.

In addition to Jenn and Katie, I have established relationships with several women who have lost loved ones to suicide. I know I can always call them if I need to talk, and vice versa. When I hear about parents who lose their young children to suicide, it flattens me. At least Tina had fifty-one years on earth. I cannot imagine losing a child to suicide. This is one of the many reasons I am heartened by Forefront. They are working so closely with schools. For three years, I was the major gifts officer for the Issaquah Schools Foundation, which supports the Issaquah School District. There were several suicides among high schoolers in the district. I emailed those school principals and encouraged them to adopt the Forefront training.

## CHAPTER 29

# Bonding over Grief

Grieving is a little bit like a buffet. Everyone chooses differently. Some eat a little, some eat a lot. Some people sit down and eat everything all at once. Others take longer with their meal and save some for later. Some even bring their leftovers home for another meal. I dug right into the grieving. I fell hard and fast, ate everything, went back for more, over and over again. My family members chose differently. My dad swallowed his grief like a large piece of meat that gets stuck in your gut and takes a long time to digest.

In March of 2015, just three months after Tina's death, Sophie had an art show in Chicago. It was her senior year at the School of the Art Institute of Chicago, and the seniors were showcasing their final project. Bill, Sylvie, Spence, Cole, Anabelle, Dad, Alexa, George and me were all set to go. A few days before the trip, Dad called me to say, "Honey, I cannot go to Chicago. My entire body is tingling, from my feet all the way up to my head. I've had several tests with no conclusion. My doctor really thinks it's my body's reaction to Tina's death. It's my way of grieving." I responded, "Ah, Dad. I understand. Take care." It made perfect sense. My father's family didn't express emotion very openly. He has never cried in front of us about Tina. His body was reacting for him.

Spencer's buffet choices were different as well. Because he is a psychiatrist, he has treated a lot of people who have been suicidal. For several years, he pleaded with Tina to stop drinking and taking Xanax. When he and I would speak, he would say, "Ingrid, Tina cannot get well until she gets sober." The night Tina died, Spencer was with his kids, Cole, and Anabelle. He didn't want to ruin New Year's for them, so he didn't tell them about Tina until the next day. He approached the buffet cautiously, and in his own timeline. As the years have passed, Spencer's anger at Tina for leaving has turned to love and to the realization that he misses her.

I would say that Alexa followed a similar pattern. On New Year's Eve, we were all calling each other. Alexa called me and fairly quickly said, "Oh great. Tina has now ruined New Year's forever." Life events have been the hardest for Alexa. She shares a birthday with Tina, so her birthday is bittersweet, every year. When their first child, Grace, was born, Eric and I went to visit them in the hospital. While I was holding Grace for the first time, Alexa's beautiful brown eyes welled up, and she said, "Ingrid, let's say a prayer for Tina. I wish she was here so, so much." Just in the past year, Alexa has started to dream more about Tina, or at least remember those dreams. Her grieving has been a few trips to the buffet line. She has eaten little bits and recently, I'd say, she has allowed herself to get bigger portions. Spence has also started to dream about her more. It's important for families to allow each member to grieve the way they need to, like choosing from a buffet. Our family did that well.

✷ ✷ ✷

In May of 2019, Eric's parents Peter and Sally Jarvis died in a car accident in Sun Valley, Idaho. On May 29th, I was coming home from a dentist appointment, and as I was nearing our driveway, I saw a police car near the entrance. The female officer rolled down her window. I asked, "May I help you?" She replied, "Yes, I am looking for the home of Dwight Jarvis." Dwight is my husband's youngest brother, and they live near us. I asked, "May I ask why?" The officer said, "I would rather not say." Dwight and Stacy have three boys, ages sixteen, nineteen, and twenty-one. I had this feeling that something had happened to one of the boys. We drove over to their driveway, and I insisted that she tell me before I knocked on their door. She repeatedly hesitated. I said, "I am not going into my sister in-law's home until I know what this is about." Then the policewoman said, "Peter and Sally Jarvis were killed in a car accident in Sun Valley Idaho this morning." Like hearing about Tina, the moment was suspended. Then I kind of collapsed; I grabbed onto the policewoman and held onto her for a bit. Peter had some sort of medical incident. He collapsed against the steering wheel, drove across the center lane of the highway. He struck a truck head on. The driver was a thirty-four-year-old young woman named Piper Reed. Piper had just finished training to become a firefighter. She was loved by many, many people in the Sun Valley region. Tragically, she was killed, along with her dog. When the emergency vehicles arrived, Peter was already dead. Sally and Piper were taken to the local hospital which was about three minutes away. They both died of injuries within thirty minutes. Peter and Sally were both eighty-two and had spent most of their lives taking care of others, their four children, and twelve grandchildren. When my husband was young, they took in foster children and unwed pregnant mothers. They were the most wonderful couple, people, parents, grandparents, and friends. I had known the Jarvis family my whole life, but after several years of being married, Sally became one of my closest friends. Their death was crushing for so many people.

Stacy and I had to call our husbands and tell them. Our thirteen-year-old dog was dying, and I knew if I asked Eric to come home, he would ask about Pele, so I had to tell him over the phone. He was on his way to a business meeting. When he picked up, I gulped and said, "Honey, I am so sorry to tell you this, but your parents were killed in a car accident this morning." There was a brief pause, and with a quivering voice, he asked, "Both of them?" He drove directly home. I met him in our garage and he fell into my arms, crying. I truly believe there was a reason I was the first person to hear about their death. I had been through a tragedy. I knew how devastated Eric and his siblings were going to be. Not being able to say goodbye is a void that can never be filled. I didn't cry for several days; I think I knew I had to be strong for Eric and our children. There were almost one thousand people at their memorial.

Upon completing this book, I asked Eric why he never really asked me about the book or my progress. He said something I needed to hear. Tina left behind such a trail of pain that he had to witness, for me, for

Bill, for their girls, my siblings, and many others. He also said, "Can you imagine how your father felt, losing his oldest child to suicide, coming to terms with that?" Eric is still angry with her and I understand. Eric, his siblings, and their parents have never really suffered from any serious depression. That condition is just not part of their gene pool. He and I have had this conversation one thousand times. He says he understands, but truly there are few people who really understood the depths of Tina's sadness, including me. Part of my healing has been to understand that everyone grieves differently and to accept their path will be different than mine. Being judgmental about someone else's process is both harmful and unproductive. I cannot begin to imagine the grief Sophie and Sylvie have endured, but their path back to wellness has humbled and inspired me.

CHAPTER 30

# The Messings

As of this writing, Sophie is twenty-eight and Sylvie is twenty-two. I couldn't love them more or be prouder of my nieces. They are reflections of Tina in every positive way. Sophie has completed coding school in Seattle and loves it. She just got a very good job in the field. She went to The School of the Art Institute of Chicago (SAIC) for college, and her expertise was printmaking. Sophie has the right-brained creative side of Tina and the left-brained, analytical side of Bill. She makes a tremendous effort to reach out to all of us and visits my mother in her home, even though Tina and my mom weren't close. Sophie is gay, and at my request, educates me about all kinds of topics like gender identity vs. sexual identity. She proudly wears a lot of Tina's jewelry and sweaters.

Sylvie looks so much like Tina that it takes my breath away. Tina was dark, and Sylvie is blonde, but the facial resemblance is amazing. She just graduated magna cum laude from Chapman University, majoring in sociology. She was the general manager of the college radio station, Chapman Radio. Sylvie loves and knows a lot about music; she recently completed an internship at a well-known label called Sub Pop. Now she works in social media at a startup. Both Sophie and Sylvie are actively involved in supporting human rights. After Tina died, Bill and Sylvie had intensive therapy, specifically in Dialectical Behavioral Therapy. A few years later, Sophie also trained in DBT. Both girls are more emotionally intelligent than most people I know. They take responsibility for their emotions, responses, and mental health. Losing Tina devastated them, but they have risen from the ashes and are remarkable women. Naturally, their compassion is strong. I give tremendous credit to Bill for ensuring his daughters got therapy. I also credit Bill's lovely wife Luisa who is their friend, but has never tried to be their mother. Tina would be so proud of them and would have delighted in their academic and creative pursuits.

After Tina died, I started to build some resentment toward Bill, feeling like he could and should have done more, specifically, reaching out to all of us for help. However, I had also been on the receiving end of Tina's bad behaviors and knew it was sometimes easier to say nothing. Bill has always been really good to me. We have a good friendship, and I care about him. When the Seattle School District hired me for my first teaching position the Sunday before Labor Day, and I was to start that Tuesday, I was so freaked out. I wanted time to set up my classroom, make a plan. I'll never forget Bill saying to me, "Ingrid, you don't have to plan the entire school year in two nights." I will always remember that comment because I was able to breathe after he said it. Essentially, Bill and I were the two people in Tina's life most familiar with her depression, and her decline. Although we may disagree about some of the details and procedures, we will always be bonded over the pain she endured and us not being able to bring her back to wellness.

Several months after Tina died, Bill started dating a lovely woman named Luisa Perticucci. Luisa is a wonderful person and truthfully, so much better suited for Bill than Tina was! They were married the fall of 2018 in Vermont. They wanted me to attend their wedding, but I told them I just couldn't. I had been the maid of honor at Tina and Bill's wedding. As much as I really like Luisa, I had a difficult time imagining Bill taking wedding vows again. It's not logical. Tina and Bill were on the verge of divorce when she died by suicide. And after Tina died, I had encouraged Bill to start dating because he and Tina had essentially been in a bad marriage for years before her death. Spence and Alexa didn't attend either. Dad made the trip though, and when I asked him why, he said, "I think it's important that I am there for Sophie and Sylvie." I have tremendous respect for Bill as a father. In the last few years of Tina's life, he was doing ninety percent of the parenting. After she died, he was everything to Sophie and Sylvie, their rock, their comfort, their provider. He joined them in many counseling sessions. He did everything a parent could and should do when their spouse dies, especially when the death is traumatic. Today the Messings are thriving, and I am in awe of how they have survived the trauma and emerged as a healthy, happy family.

# CHAPTER 31

# Goodbye

Seven years later, there are still so many days when the only person I want to talk to is Tina. Donald Trump would have been marvelous fodder for her humor. She would have written beautifully about the COVID-19 Pandemic, the isolation, grief, loss, fear, and the general fatigue felt by the whole world. While she was well, her mind was so quick, agile. My biggest regret is that I should have shown more compassion toward Tina during her struggle with addiction and depression, and less judgment, especially during the last two years. I wanted her to get better so badly that I pushed her and nagged her, instead of just being there for her. Now I wish I had just held her hand, snuggled up with her, and said, "I am so sorry you are in so much pain. It must feel so lonely and hard. I am here for you in whatever capacity you need me to be."

If you know someone who has debilitating depression and you are concerned about them, absolutely do what you can to get them professional help. Also understand that chronic pain, whether it's physical, mental, or emotional, takes an unrelenting toll on a human. Depression doesn't always have a root cause, particularly if it's chemical depression. I have done so much soul-searching about this. For some people, being on planet Earth is just too hard. I don't mean to sound callous, but I understand now that taking her life was the only way Tina believed she could find peace. And I have found peace in this. It was five years before I could make myself go into the Four Seasons Hotel.

One of my favorite places is the Seattle Children's PlayGarden, a wonderful indoor/outdoor preschool that is a school for children of all abilities. They hold their annual luncheon at the Four Seasons Hotel. I hadn't been there since Tina died, but about a year ago, my sweet Hazel held my hand, and we walked into the lobby. I was expecting a thunderbolt of grief, but I did not experience that. The hotel does not hold Tina's spirit. All of us who loved her do.

I have recurring dreams about Tina. One is that on Christmas morning I have forgotten to give her a present, which I never forgot in our lifetime. Perhaps the present symbolizes the gift of compassion that I didn't give enough of. Another dream is that Tina lives in New York City, has a secret life away from all of us, a boyfriend and a career. In this dream, she is always quiet and incredibly serene. She clearly wants her distance from us and she is happy. This one is my favorite dream.

Toward the end of writing this memoir, I became frustrated and doubted everything about it. Should I have even written it? Have I been able to give the reader an accurate picture of the complex and beautiful woman Tina was? Have I been honest about the fact that we loved each other, but that there were also a lot of struggles? Then, I realized this is my story about me and my sister. It is as authentic as I know it to be. Her story would have been different, and I am confident that it would have been better written and funnier than mine. That's OK. I needed a way to process the last seven years. I am grateful for the experience and the opportunity to go way back in time and relive many, many moments with her. I wanted our life's journey to continue together, but Tina had a different plan. Tina, if you are floating around up there, cracking jokes, speaking Mandarin, making jewelry, know that there was never anyone who loved you more than I loved you. I am sorry for sometimes doing things that hurt you. I cherish and honor the incredible person you were. Thank you for being my lioness, my funny sister, the one person who knew me better than anyone. For my solace, I choose to see your humor in Henry, your dark beauty in George, and your playfulness in Hazel. Our family will continue to lovingly watch over Sophie and Sylvie. Save me a spot at the witches' stove or anywhere we can play and laugh together.

My shrine to Tina

Bill, Sophie, Sylvie at
Sophie's art show

Family at Sophie's art show

Alexa and me

Page holding Grace

Bill and Luisa's wedding

Sophie and Sylvie

Spencer, Cole, Anabelle Helsell

Mark, Alexa, Grace, Bo McIntyre

Henry, Eric, Ingrid, George, Hazel Jarvis

## ACKNOWLEDGMENTS

Robert Helsell-who lost his oldest daughter

Spencer and Alexa Helsell-my cherished brother and sister

Bill Messing-for incredible parenting and for loving Tina

Sophie and Sylvie Messing-the lights in Tina's life

Luisa Perticucci-Bills' wife and friend to Sophie and Sylvie

Page MacDonald-for the care she has given our family and our friendship

Emily Mora-for the love and protection she has given to Sophie and Sylvie

Catherine Monk-for her love for Tina and her work with pregnancy and depression

Sally Schwartz-for her friendship with Tina and providing the Cayman Islands

Linda Cline-for their lifelong friendship and caring of Tina

Members of the Tina Helsell Guild-for your support of Tina and me

Katie Simmons and Jenn Stuber-for Forefront and your presence

My wonderful friends-for always being there for me

The Jarvis Family-for stability, love, nine adored nieces, nephews, and two great nieces

Henry, George, and Hazel- my treasures who guided me through the darkest time in my life

My love Eric- for the life you have provided, your confidence in me, and teaching me resilience